Advanced Team Facilitation

*Tools to
Achieve
High
Performance
Teams*

*Written by
Ingrid Bens M.Ed.*

Advanced Team Facilitation
Tools to Achieve High Performance Teams

Advanced Team Facilitation was originally published as *Teams in Trouble: Strategies to Help Teams with Problems,* written by Ingrid Bens 1998.

Development Team

Writer
Ingrid Bens, M.Ed.

Editor
Michael Goldman

Revisions
Carolyn Field

Cover
Michele Kierstead

Typography
Mary House

GOAL/QPC

2 Manor Parkway, Salem, NH 03079-2841

Toll free: 800-643-4316
Fax: 603-870-9122
Web site: www.goalqpc.com

Phone: 603-890-8800
E-mail: service@goalqpc.com

Printed in the United States of America
First Edition
9 8 7 6 5 4 3 2 1
ISBN 1-57681-034-8 (perfect bound)
ISBN 1-57681-033-X (spiral bound)
(Previously published by Participative Dynamics, ISBN 1-890416-01-0)

Table of Contents

Introduction

In today's high pressure workplace, every team needs to be productive. That's why every team leader needs to be able to recognize and know how to make interventions that resolve the most common team dysfunctions. This book provides insights into typical team problems, plus practical strategies, tools, and techniques for getting them back on track.

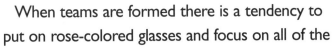

When teams are formed there is a tendency to put on rose-colored glasses and focus on all of the benefits. Too often there's no recognition of the well-documented fact that all teams should expect at least one *storming* episode during their development. During this predictable stage, members become disenchanted and conflicts are commonplace.

Because most leaders aren't prepared for storming, lots of teams don't survive it. This is both unfortunate and unnecessary since team conflicts can be overcome by implementing preventative measures and by making appropriate and timely interventions.

> *The problem isn't that teams get into trouble*
> *– that's to be expected! The real problem*
> *is that team difficulties are too often ignored.*

When a team gets into trouble, it can easily sink deeper and deeper into misery. What might have been an easy problem to solve had it been caught early, turns into a major stumbling block. Eventually the problems deepen, people stop communicating, and energy levels drop. Without the proper intervention, the team will most likely become increasingly ineffective, run out of energy, or disintegrate.

> *All team leaders need strategies for*
> *managing team problems.*

This manual is written for team leaders and is based on years of experience helping real teams get back on track. What's unique about this workbook is that it offers detailed steps any leader can use to diagnose and resolve team problems. This book can of course, also be used by facilitators, consultants, and trainers who are brought in to help, from outside the team.

On the pages that follow you'll learn:

- how to recognize the main sources of team problems
- how to use data gathering tools and techniques
- how to make immediate interventions
- the steps in making a planned intervention
- the techniques and attitudes needed to make every intervention a success
- preventative strategies for avoiding major 'storms.'

This manual also contains step-by-step intervention outlines for the twelve most commonly encountered team problems.

While hundreds of books have been written about teams, we have noticed that most explain the team concept or deal with the initial team building process. In spite of the need, there's a real lack of information and training about how to anticipate, avoid and resolve typical team problems. It has been our experience that these skills are needed now!

We know you'll find this book to be a valuable resource in creating more resilient and effective teams!

Ingrid Bens, M.Ed.

Why Teams Get into Trouble

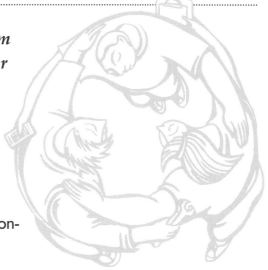

Anyone who has ever been on a team knows only too well how easy it is for any team to get itself into trouble.

When a new team gets started, things are usually very positive: energy levels are high, members are on their best behavior, the leader seems reasonable and the organization is pledging its support. There may even be a 'honeymoon' feeling in the air.

Unfortunately, for most teams reality soon sets in. While a few teams may be able to sail through life without facing serious difficulties, most encounter problems sooner or later. The likelihood of experiencing difficulties is so great, in fact, that it's been given the name *storming*, and has become recognized as a predictable stage of any team's development. That's why every team leader needs to be armed with strategies for navigating turbulent waters.

> *At some time or other your team is going to experience 'storming' so you'd better be ready to intervene!*

Benchmarking Against a High Performance Team

Before we explore the nature of team problems, it's important to know what an effective high performance team looks like and how your team compares. Use the following five-point rating scale to assess your team's current level of health.

1 = poor   2 = fair   3 = satisfactory   4 = good   5 = excellent

 A team that is performing effectively has:

____ Members who know each other well and work cooperatively with a spirit of teamwork and respect

____ A clear picture of who the team's customers are, plus a clear understanding of their needs and expectations

A team that is performing effectively has:

____ A clear goal that the members feel a strong commitment to achieving together

____ Specific objectives and results indicators that define exactly how the team goal will be achieved

____ Well-defined roles and responsibilities so that every member knows their specific commitments and how to link with others

____ A detailed empowerment plan that spells out which decisions the team can make on its own and which they need approval for

____ Balanced work plans/project plans that include critical paths and a means of follow-up to ensure that action items are implemented

____ A regular time and place for team meetings that all members are committed to attending

____ Effective meetings that have detailed agendas, are well managed, fully attended, and productive

____ A profile of member skills that helps people access each others' expertise

____ A training plan for each individual member, as well as one for the team as a whole

____ A set of team rules, created by the members, that describes the behaviors and values by which members agree to conduct themselves

____ Members who have highly developed interpersonal skills and who exhibit listening and supporting behaviors

____ Highly developed facilitation skills amongst all members who take turns managing team process at meetings

____ Skill at managing conflict and making tough decisions without anger or division

____ Open lines of communication and good relations with customers, other teams and the rest of the organization

____ Regularly scheduled evaluation and feedback activities designed to improve both individual and team performance

____ An empowering leader who deliberately shares leadership responsibilities with others and acts like a coach

____ A positive, responsible, and committed attitude amongst team members

____ An appropriate means of rewarding achievement and celebrating success

When a team exhibits these traits, it's a pleasure to be a member. People offer their ideas, support each other, and produce results. Power is shared and everyone has a sense that their skills are being enhanced by being on the team. This is how a true team functions and feels.

The good news is that lots of teams do achieve this state. The bad news is that many more never get there because no one steps in to fix things when they go wrong!

Learning to Spot Team Problems

Team problems come in all types and sizes. These problems can center on just one person or they can involve the whole group. Teams can experience problems related to their processes, such as the techniques they use to make decisions. Teams can also encounter problems dealing with other teams, their work or with the rest of the organization.

Read through the following scenarios to identify if any of these are present in your team:

____ Some people act as if they wish they weren't on the team

____ Different members seem to be working towards different goals

____ Some members are confused about the goal of the team

____ Meetings are poorly planned and members seem unprepared

____ Few items at any meeting are brought to closure

____ A great deal of time is wasted at meetings

____ Too many decisions are made by one or two dominant members

____ The team uses voting in many situations when it should be striving to reach consensus

____ The same people bicker with each other at every meeting, while others sit in embarrassed silence

____ One of the team's members has appointed himself as 'devil's advocate,' spending their time shooting down ideas

____ Members use inappropriate language and argue emotionally with each other any time there's a difference of opinion

____ Discussions often turn into arguments

____ Everyone just ignores conflict and prays it will go away

____ Conversations often go off-track and no one brings them back

____ Conflicts end when one side gives in

____ When topics are being discussed, people seem reluctant to speak their minds

____ Some members sit passively and say nothing at meetings

____ After team meetings there are lots of complaints

____ Time is wasted fighting over resources or territory, either within the team or with other teams

____ Members don't say what they really think when the leader is in the room

____ There are frequent meetings that exclude the leader

____ Some team members seem to be engaged in a power struggle to take the lead

____ Some people really work hard, while others do little

____ There isn't consistent follow-through on action plans

____ The leader micro-manages members by insisting on examining every minute detail of every assignment

____ A few members openly challenge whatever ideas the leader puts forward

____ No one seems sure of the priorities anymore

____ There is cynicism that the organization isn't supporting the team concept

____ After many months of high energy, the team seems to be running out of steam

> *If you're seeing one or more of these scenarios,*
> *you need to make an intervention to get*
> *your team back on track!*

So Why do Teams Get into Trouble?

Teams flounder for a complex set of reasons. From our observations these reasons include:

#1. Teams are made up of people. This makes it inevitable that someone will eventually rub someone else the wrong way. On top of that, some people lack interpersonal skills. Still others may want to control the team. The potential sources of interpersonal conflict are endless!

#2. Some people really aren't cut out for teams. They may be extremely intro-verted, anti-social, or just want to stay in the safety of the job they're comfortable with.

#3. Leading a team is different from managing or supervising a department. A lot of new team leaders don't understand the differences. As a result, some leaders may use an autocratic approach, against which members eventually rebel.

#4. Teamwork is more complex than working alone. Every decision needs to be discussed. Reaching consensus is a challenge and people have to coordinate their roles much more than they probably did in the past. Teamwork also demands lots of time spent in meetings. These frustrations can build into conflict.

#5. Being on a team takes highly developed interpersonal, meeting, and facili-tation skills. Lack of adequate training in these important areas sets the stage for dysfunctional behavior and wasted time.

#6. The workplace is full of stress these days. People are under tremendous work pressure, on top of their responsibilities at home. This means that people may react negatively when asked to take on more responsibility.

#7. Many companies are experiencing an unfortunate atmosphere of cyni-cism and uncertainty from years of cutbacks and layoffs. In these organizations, employee trust is at an all time low. Because teams are often formed to improve pro-ductivity, cynical members can view teamwork as yet another tactic to extract more work from an already stretched work force.

#8. Most organizations don't adjust their culture to really empower. The result is that teams often feel their progress is being blocked, which can lead to disillusion-ment and even strife.

#9. Vague organization charts can set teams up to compete with other teams for turf or scarce resources.

#10. Teams need to be launched properly. They need a clear goal, measurable objectives, rules of conduct and well defined roles and responsibilities. If a team just jumps into its task without establishing these parameters, it's likely to experience con-fusion and wasted efforts later on.

In addition to all of the above, teams are predisposed to periodic episodes of *storming*. Storming is a natural stage of team development that's characterized by member dissatisfaction and conflict. In addition to storming, about any of the items mentioned above, power struggles with the leader or between members are common place.

Your first step in being able to deal with teams in trouble is to learn about the natural life cycle of teams.

Know the Team Development Stages

Team problems are a lot easier to deal with once you understand that teams go through a series of growth stages and that each stage demands the use of different leadership strategies. Team development starts with:

Forming – The Honeymoon Stage

When a team is first brought together, it's said to be in *forming*. At this stage, people feel both excited about the new venture and anxious about the unknown. The members may not know each other, so there's natural shyness. It's quite common for new team members to worry that they won't be accepted by the others. Wanting to make a good impression, most members will be on their best behavior. It's also not uncommon for people to hold back and adopt a 'wait and see' attitude during start-up.

A shy and uncertain phase when members are checking each other out and in need of direction about where the team is going.

During forming, the team's task is at the idea stage, so everyone is still optimistic. The realities of getting the job done haven't sunk in yet, so people usually feel positive and challenged about what's ahead.

Because of new team jitters, most new teams exhibit an over-dependence on the leader. This is especially true if the members have previously worked for an autocratic manager or been in highly structured jobs. Past dependency makes most members experience the start-up phase as a time of ambiguity. They expect their leader to relieve their unease by providing a clear mandate, structure and parameters. At this point, members want and need their leader to be 'in charge.'

Leading a Team That's in Forming

Since new team members are feeling unsure and somewhat shy, the leader of a *forming* team needs to act friendly, open and reassuring, plus:

__ make sure there's clarity about the mandate and parameters of the new team

__ help members collaborate to create a goal that achieves the mandate

__ break the ice with activities that create comfort and disclosure

__ be encouraging and empowering

__ help members develop norms or rules of conduct

__ identify tasks, as well as specific roles and responsibilities

__ provide structure for all discussions and meetings

__ manage participation so that everyone has an equal say

__ set a tone of openness and trust

__ provide training in decision-making and effective behaviors

In the forming stage, the best leadership strategy to encourage member independence is to adopt a *facilitative* rather than *directive* approach. This ensures that members contribute their ideas and commitment. This approach provides structure, while at the same time actively involves members in defining their new team.

Since there usually isn't a lot of conflict or serious trouble at the forming stage, members tend to feel they're on a sort of 'honeymoon.'

Forming is, however, a major turning point. If the leader handles the forming stage well and helps the team establish a solid foundation with clear goals, measurable objectives, rules of conduct and so forth, forming should be short, structured and followed directly by a period of effective team performance.

If, on the other hand, the leader doesn't understand what members need and lets the team plunge into doing its work without properly setting the context, this alone can throw the team into storming. If the storming issues are serious and remain unaddressed, they may drag the team down or even destroy it.

Because properly launching a team is such a critical step, we have devoted a whole resource manual to the subject called – *Team Launch: Strategies for Leaders of New*

Teams. It outlines the ten components that every team needs to work through in order to complete a proper launch and provides worksheets, overheads, and step-by-step facilitator notes for running an actual team launch session. A brief summary of this team launch process is described on page 42.

Storming – the 'Make or Break It' Stage

As its name suggests, storming is a tempestuous time. Gone are the calm waters of forming. The team starts encountering the realities of getting the job done. Team mates may start disliking each other and interpersonal conflicts may develop. Because this strife weighs on people's minds, it distracts the team from focusing on getting the job done. As a result, productivity declines during storming. This leads to a feeling that the team is 'spinning its wheels.' As frustration increases, there is usually a corresponding deterioration in morale.

A stage characterized by disillusionment, frustration, and conflict in which problems distract the members from its task.

Depending on how severe storming gets, people may even start to wonder if they can find a way to leave the team.

Leading Effectively During Storming

Storming is the most challenging stage of team development. If it's handled effectively, the members will address their problems, resolve them, and move forward. If, on the other hand, problems are ignored or mismanaged, storming can be the beginning of the end of the team.

This manual has been written to help you avoid disaster, by providing clear steps and methods with which to respond to storming. These techniques are described in-depth, starting on page 40.

As team leader you shouldn't let storming throw you. It's best to:

✓ expect and accept tensions as normal

✓ stay totally calm and neutral

✓ create an atmosphere where people can safely express feelings

✓ openly admit that there's conflict

✓ help members identify issues

✓ invite input and feedback

✓ assertively facilitate heated discussions

✓ train members in group skills

✓ encourage open and clear communication

There's no schedule by which to predict when a team will enter storming. If the team's launch is mismanaged and there's a lack of clarity about the goal, confusion about roles or a lack of rules, storming can start right during the first team meeting!

If, on the other hand, the team starts with a thorough launch discussion, conducted by a facilitative leader who has some basic team skills training, storming will be minimal In this scenario the team sails out of forming, right into a period of effective performance. While such a team might encounter storming phases later in its life, a well grounded team will be able to deal with these periodic episodes in a constructive manner.

> *The bottom-line is that sooner or later every team will storm. Storming can be either:*
>
> | early, prolonged, and debilitating, if problems are ignored or mismanaged | *or* | delayed, short, cathartic and a source of team improvement if properly diagnosed and managed. |
> | --- | --- | --- |

Adopting the right attitude and taking a proactive approach will be the critical factors in determining which of these storming scenarios plays out for your team!

Leading Effectively During Storming

Storming is very much about control. During storming, it's common for members to feel dissatisfied with their dependence on the team's official leader. It's so common for members to challenge the leader at this stage, that battles over power are regarded as a reliable sign that the team has indeed entered storming. Power struggles aren't limited to the leader either – members will often vie for power with each other, or will even do battle with the organization.

Understanding that this stage is normal, much like an adolescent period, should make it easier to not take the conflicts and rebellion personally. As the leader you will lose your ability to handle storming if you let yourself think:

> *This is awful – things are falling apart!*
>
> *They hate me – well, I hate them too!*
>
> *I can't trust them!*
>
> *Who do they think they are?*
>
> *I'll fix them!*

Instead, you need to adopt a calm and positive mindset. Tell yourself:

> *Storming is ok... it's a normal stage.*
>
> *They don't hate me... they're just storming!*
>
> *They don't hate each other... they're just storming!*
>
> *This is energy I've got to channel into solutions.*
>
> *I've got to find the right intervention to get us through this together!*

As mentioned earlier, the tools and techniques for handling storming follow this discussion on team stages. For now, the things to remember about this most difficult stage are:

- storming is a normal developmental stage that can happen at any time: early in the life of the team, and/or later on in repeat episodes

- as team leader, you can reduce the severity of storming by using preventative strategies like providing training and conducting a thorough team launch process

- it's always better to face storming whenever it happens, rather than avoiding and letting things fester

Norming - A Time for Settling Disputes

Norming happens when the team faces its problems and resolves them. The solutions that members agree to, become the new rules or *norms* for the team.

A transitionary step that moves the team out of storming into the final stage, performing.

You should note that norming is not about the leader stepping in to dictate to the team how they should handle their challenges. This would be directive and would regress the team to a point where members are once again dependent on the leader. The trick about managing norming the right way is to facilitate it, so that the intervention is actually made by the members themselves.

Norming is a period of making planned interventions. It's a very active and challenging time for the leader whose role is to design and implement the right activities to actively engage members in resolving their team's problems.

> *You exit storming and enter the norming phase when you support members in resolving their problems.*

In norming, members are helped to face their issues, accept feedback and act on it. The result of dealing with issues and removing barriers is that the team's performance improves.

In this manual we refer to major norming activities as planned interventions. In our experience there are six different types of planned interventions. Each intervention type responds to a specific set of circumstances.

1. Re-form the Team

If the team is storming because it was never properly launched in the first place, go back to the launch stage and clarify the goal, objectives, rules, roles and responsibilities, team processes, etc., to bring needed structure to the team's operations.

2. Provide Training

If the team is in trouble because members lack basic meeting, technical, or interpersonal skills, identify training needs and then provide workshops or other learning opportunities for members.

3. Identify and Solve Team Problems

If the team is being blocked by the organization or is experiencing internal problems, help the members identify and systematically problem-solve these issues.

4. Share Feedback

If meetings, team and/or individual performance are declining, implement feedback activities that give members the data they need to make improvements.

5. Coach Individual Members

If individuals are letting the rest of the team down because of poor personal work habits, use coaching to encourage performance improvement.

6. Mediate Conflicts

If two members or two parties are feuding and no longer cooperating, use third party intervention techniques to help members overcome strife.

Starting on page 40 you will find a detailed description and the tools needed to conduct each of the six aforementioned planned interventions.

The Leader's Role in Norming

Your most important role in norming is to make timely use of the right methodology to match the team's problem. As in storming, it's essential that you be totally neutral and focus on managing the process. Key actions include:

✓ creating the right atmosphere that supports people in facing up to problems

✓ encouraging identification and solving of problems

✓ offering and accepting personal feedback

✓ helping members gain new skills

✓ supporting members while they make improvements

✓ further sharing of power

✓ encouraging others to take on leadership roles

Performing – The Final Team Growth Stage

If norming is managed successfully, the team will transition to a period of improved performance in which members can focus on their work without distraction. As a result, productivity goes up and so does morale.

A period of high productivity and effectiveness in which members display high levels of commitment to both each other and to the team's task.

In high performing teams, power is shared by rotating leadership responsibilities. People take turns facilitating discussions and leading projects. They start to rely on each other. The official leader of a high performance team is treated like a valued member. Everyone behaves in a cooperative manner and there's lots of mutual support. The team evaluates and corrects continuously. Members feel committed and bonded.

A high performance team is one that has evolved to the point where it makes quality decisions and uses its time and resources efficiently. Conflicts still happen, but they're experienced as constructive debates. Things rarely get heated or overly emotional.

As team leader it's your job to get your team to the performing stage as quickly as possible and then make sure it stays there!

Leading a Team in the Performing Stage

Performing is the final stage of team development and the easiest to lead. By now members have greatly improved their interpersonal skills and have learned to manage their own conflicts.

With your team at the performing stage, your role is far less stressful or active than at the earlier stages. Members are now providing a lot of leadership to each other. At this stage your best strategies are to:

✓ collaborate with members to get their input

✓ encourage members to take on greater responsibilities

✓ share leadership roles like facilitating meetings

✓ offer your expertise to the team

✓ help the team structure its work

✓ act as buffer or 'go between' with the rest of the organization

✓ serve as coach and adviser to the team and also to individual members

✓ provide training

✓ facilitate on-going team improvement activities

✓ help the team reward and celebrate success

✓ be ready to facilitate interventions at the first signs of trouble

The leader of any team in performing always has to:

1. Stay alert to the potential for storming, no matter how effectively the team appears to be behaving.

2. Remember that episodes of storming can occur at any time.

3. Acknowledge that it's the job of the leader to know the signs of trouble and be ready to make the appropriate intervention.

> *Even when a team has reached performing it can still experience episodes of storming.*

Leader Strategies Chart

Use the following quick reference to match appropriate leadership activities with team development stages.

Stage	Key Features	Appropriate Strategies
Forming	Members unsure	Warm-up exercises
	Uncertainty	Disclosure exercises
	Low trust	Build buy-in
	Need direction	Create a common goal
	Commitment low	Create and use norms
	Group skills unrefined	Define accountabilities
	Overdependence on leader	Clarify roles and responsibilities
		Provide clear process
		Encourage participation
		Provide training

Main Strategy – Build team spirit and comfort while providing lots of structure for activities

Stage	Key Elements	Appropriate Strategies
Storming	Conflict emerges	Expect and accept tension
	Frustration sets in	Stay neutral and calm
	Animosities develop	Create safety for expressing feelings
	Emotional arguing	Honestly admit there's conflict
	Cliques form	Help members identify issues
	Leader is rejected	Invite input and feedback
	Issues emerge	Diagnose intervention needs
	Power struggles	Assertively referee conflict
		Make immediate interventions
		Encourage communication

Main Strategy – To listen, address conflict, referee assertively

Leader Strategies Chart, cont'd

Stage	Key Elements	Appropriate Strategies
Norming	Members 'own' problems Conflicts are resolved Power issues are resolved Team redefines its norms Performance problems are corrected Empowerment is redefined	Offer methods for feedback Help solve problems Invite personal feedback Offer further training Support members while they make improvements Share power Mediate personality clashes Coach and counsel individuals Share the leadership role

*Main Strategy — To facilitate interventions
and implement improvements*

Stage	Key Elements	Appropriate Strategies
Performing	High productivity Conflicts managed by members Commitment to goal high Roles and responsibilities clear Members behave in a facilitative manner Team continuously improves itself Members feel committed and bonded	Collaborate with members on process Rotate facilitation duties Offer your expertise Help the team recognize and celebrate success

*Main strategy — Build agendas together, share facilitation
responsibilities, collaborate, act as a resource*

How the Stages Take Place

The following diagrams provide some additional insight into how the development stages might evolve.

Scenario #1 – the theory of team development maintains that the four stages happen in sequence. Since storming is a period of distraction for the team, its ability to get work done is impaired and hence there is a dip in productivity. The following diagram assumes that the team resolves its problems in due course.

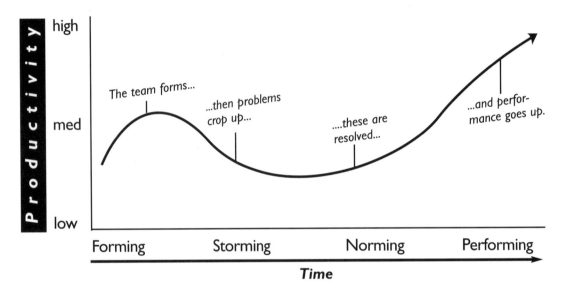

Scenario #2 – this diagram tells the sad (and all too common) story of a team that did not get launched properly. When interpersonal clashes arose, issues were ignored and problems festered. Because the team never stopped to address its troubles, it entered a long period of storming and finally died.

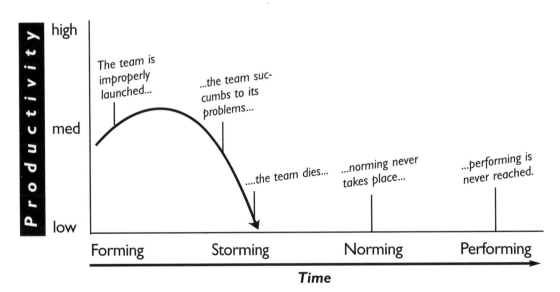

Scenario #3 – this diagram illustrates what we've observed to be the way the stages of team development usually unfold. It shows that storming isn't a one-time occurrence, but actually recurs over and over during the life of the team. It also shows that teams can experience relatively high performance early on. This scenario is dependent on there having been adequate training for both the leader and the team members. This scenario also assumes that the leader knows how to identify the signs of trouble and make the right interventions in a timely fashion.

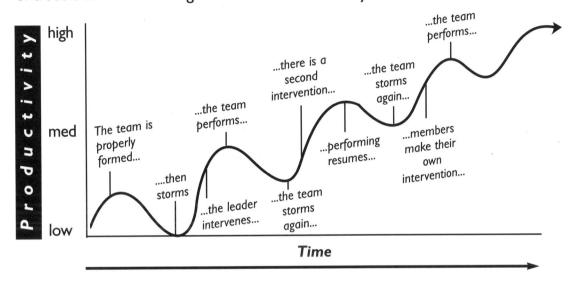

In scenario #3 the periods of storming get smaller each time the team goes through a successful intervention. Once a team has learned to overcome its problems, it's much easier to make interventions again. In fact, some teams become so comfortable and skilled at identifying and solving problems that they norm routinely as a preventative measure. When a team reaches this level of mastery over its internal processes, storming periods are light and infrequent.

Our Goal for You

The aim of this book is to get you on the path to team development depicted in scenario #3. We want you to conduct a thorough launch process, then move directly into a period of effective performance, with only a few minor storms along the way.

When storming does take place, we want you to be able to handle each episode quickly. To do this you need to be armed with the right intervention strategies to surface issues and get your team back to a high performance state.

Is Your Team in Trouble?

All team leaders need to be on the alert for signs of trouble. The sooner you spot a problem and deal with it, the better. Use the following checklist to help build your awareness of the types of situations where an intervention may be necessary. You will note that the checklist of symptoms has been organized to match the six types of interventions as identified in this workbook.

Type #1. The Team Needs to Re-form

____ The purpose of the team is unclear and members periodically express confusion about the priorities.

____ There are no clear rules to guide member conduct at meetings.

____ Members are unsure about which decisions they can make and which need management approval.

____ The team isn't sure which customers, processes, or products are their priority.

____ There are no clear objectives or measures to guide team efforts.

____ Members seem unclear about exactly who is doing what or how to make maximum use of each other's skills.

____ There is no clear communication plan in place.

Type #2. The Team Needs Training

____ Meetings seem to waste a lot of time.

____ Agendas lack good planning and too few items are brought to satisfactory closure.

____ There's confusion about decision-making, as the team overuses voting or has difficulty achieving consensus.

____ Objectivity is leaving debates, as people bicker and generally exhibit dysfunctional behavior.

____ Too many discussions seem to go in circles and off-track.

____ There's seldom a clear process for how to tackle a discussion, systematically analyze a situation, or solve a problem.

____ Members lack the ability to facilitate discussions.

____ Some members lack the technical skills to get their job done.

Type #3. The Team Needs to Identify and Solve Problems

____ People seem to be holding back during meetings, then meeting after to discuss the real problems in 'closed door' sessions.

____ The team is not effective at completing its action plans.

____ People outside the team, who rely on its work, are dissatisfied with the team's performance.

____ Everyone seems totally overwhelmed by their individual workload.

____ The important priorities of the team don't seem to be getting done.

____ Team progress is being hampered by factors from outside the team.

____ Members constantly complain about, or are oblivious to a variety of internal issues, but these are never tackled systematically and resolved.

Type #4. Team Members Need to Share Feedback

____ Some people don't say or do much, appearing to be 'along for the ride,' while a few hardworking members do all the work.

____ One or more of the team's members have assumed the role of critic, as ideas are put down before they're really explored and understood.

____ Members make cutting remarks and aim innuendoes at each other during meetings.

____ People act as if they were harboring grudges about past events.

____ Between meetings most members complain to each other about the leader whose style is seen as ineffective.

____ The team seems to do its best work when the leader isn't there.

Type #5. An Individual Needs Coaching

____ One person is repeatedly letting down the rest of the team and not completing assignments on time.

____ The work of one member is consistently below expectations.

Type #6. There's a Conflict to Mediate

____ Two or more members of the team seem to be engaged in a power struggle for control of the team. Neither one supports the ideas put forward by the other. Outside of meetings they each try to build up their personal support.

____ The team has split into cliques, with little cooperation between the factions.

____ Two or more members of the team are embroiled in a long-standing conflict that they play out during team meetings.

____ Your team seems engaged in a small 'war' over resources and turf with another team.

These scenarios are, of course, just a sample of the real life problems that teams encounter. Without correction, any one of these issues can threaten the future of the team. Each problem demands that you intervene in a timely manner. To help you further assess your team's situation, use the assessment sheet that follows.

Assessment Worksheet

Thinking about your own team:

What troubling symptoms are you noticing?

What do you guess to be the underlying causes of these symptoms?

What stage of development would you say the team is in now *(forming, storming, norming or performing)*?

How would you describe your leadership approach up until now?

What has been tried so far to resolve the situation? What has been the outcome of these efforts?

The Critical Role of the Leader

While there may be some teams that are able to reach high performance with a poor leader, it's generally true that the success of a team depends on whether or not the leader has the right skills and attitudes for the job.

In many ways, teams are more sensitive to the quality of their leaders than are normal work units or departments. We've all had inept bosses whom we learned to work around. While a poor manager may have been able to keep his/her department running year after year, he/she wouldn't have likely been able to build a high performance team using those same skills and tactics. That's because teams demand a different approach.

Why are Teams More of a Challenge?

For starters, team leaders have to manage 'relationships' much more than traditional supervisors. Teams are also more interpersonally intense than traditional departments, where employees focus on doing the work within their personal job description. Teams demand much more collaboration and cooperation. There are shared objectives to fulfill and roles to coordinate, which

When your team is in trouble, there's more than a slight chance the problem could be you!

means more meetings and more assignments that force people to work together. With all this increased interaction, there's more potential for conflict. In short, managing a team is more about managing relationships than it is about supervising work.

For these and other reasons, successfully leading a team demands a significant shift in leadership style. While it may be possible to manage a department in a controlling way, no team will ever mature past the *forming* stage unless its leader shifts to a more facilitative, empowering, coaching style. As many new team leaders have found out, this is easier said than done.

Anyone about to lead a team needs to understand the necessary shifts in both leadership style and role. Reading at least a few of the hundreds of books available on team leadership is a good idea. So is taking a team leadership training course that teaches its participants how to facilitate and use group process tools.

The sad truth is that too few leaders are properly prepared for their new role and approach it with the same frame of mind they used when supervising or managing in the past. Because of this, a surprisingly high proportion of team troubles are directly related to the leader's lack of preparation and skill.

How Leaders Create Team Problems

To make sure that you don't end up being *the cause* of your team's ultimate demise, we provide the following illustrations of the ways we have seen leaders bring havoc to their teams. Unfortunately, each of the following represents real situations we've encountered.

To Ensure Disaster:

1. Rule with a firm hand. Let them know you're the boss. Spell out your expectations and punish those who don't conform.

2. Keep important information to yourself: only let people know what you think they need to know.

3. Discourage people from disagreeing with you, especially in front of others at meetings.

4. Keep changing your opinion on key issues to 'keep 'em guessing.'

5. Never give or accept feedback about your performance as leader.

6. Divide and conquer: encourage factions and fuel their fires.

7. Never help members resolve their conflicts.

8. Make all outside team presentations yourself and make sure your name is on all team reports.

9. Attend all team meetings. Never let people meet without you.

10. Check everything yourself: know all the details and play the 'devil's advocate' with everyone's work to keep them on their toes.

11. Pick favorites and mentor them: groom these people to succeed you.

12. Chair all the team meetings and maintain personal control over the development of all team agendas.

13. Take all team problems 'off-line' to solve them behind closed doors.

To Ensure Success:

In contrast to the foregoing formula for disaster, we offer the following formulas for success. Please remember that a truly thorough discussion of effective leadership is beyond the scope of this book and we urge you to seek out more information on this critically important topic.

1. Gain an understanding of how teams are different from regular work groups and know the growth stages teams go through.

2. Seek training in facilitation skills, as well as customer service, coaching, conflict mediation, meeting management, and the use of process improvement tools.

3. Brush up your own interpersonal skills such as giving and receiving feedback, active listening, paraphrasing, supporting, and encouraging.

4. Adopt the right mind-set: namely, that the team is now your customer and that your job is to support its members. Abandon the notion that these people work for you and that you're the 'boss.'

5. Become a communicator and a networker to link your team to others. Share information relentlessly.

6. Become a 'boundary' manager who actively works on behalf of the team with both senior management and other teams.

7. Share power: encourage others to manage meetings, make tough decisions and take the lead. Encourage members to take the spotlight.

8. Empower people so that they have enough authority to make decisions and are able to take independent action.

9. Make sure the team is properly launched and is always operating within a clear framework.

10. Implement regular feedback exercises so that the team assesses its meetings, as well as its own effectiveness. Also institute periodic peer and leader feedback sessions to make self-improvement a part of the team's culture.

11. Become an active coach for both individuals and the team as a whole. Always work on trying to help the team improve itself and its service to its customers.

12. Always recognize and reward people's contributions. Celebrate every victory together.

To test your personal effectiveness, you can take the leadership effectiveness self-test on the pages that follow. You can also re-word each question slightly and have your team members anonymously answer the survey about you. That lets you benefit from their insights about your effectiveness as a leader.

Team Leadership Self-Assessment

Review the following and check off those statements that fairly reflect your present leadership practices. Leave blank any statements that don't apply.

Use this scale to rate each question:

1. *I don't do this at all or I am totally unaware of this*
2. *I don't do this much or I am somewhat unaware of this*
3. *Not sure*
4. *I do this somewhat or I am somewhat aware of this*
5. *I do this all the time or I am totally aware of this*

1. ___ I understand that teams go through phases and that I need to adjust my approach to match the skills and attitudes of team members.

2. ___ I have a good understanding of how to shift my personal style to be a more empowering and facilitative leader.

3. ___ I think of team members as my partners and valuable resources.

4. ___ I have a good grasp of fundamental facilitation skills and the use of process tools.

5. ___ I know how to plan and manage meetings so that they're efficient and effective.

6. ___ I am familiar with the key decision-making tools and which to use in which situations.

7. ___ I understand that teams go through a storming phase and accept the potential for conflict as a normal aspect of team life.

8. ___ I see conflict as a positive opportunity. I don't ignore or suppress it.

9. ___ I'm a good listener and supporter of other people's ideas.

10. ___ Whenever possible I empower team members to make decisions and take responsibility.

11. ___ I make sure there is a steady flow of information to my team at all times.

12. ____ I encourage team members to independently find and solve problems.

13. ____ I don't dominate meetings with my ideas, but hold back and encourage others to participate.

14. ____ Whenever there's an important decision to be made, I encourage discussion and the use of consensus to arrive at a final decision.

15. ____ I ensure that the team has a clear goal and that members know exactly which objectives and results they're accountable for.

16. ____ I make sure the team has a clear set of rules. We post and use these rules to help us manage our meetings.

17. ____ I spend time with each person quarterly to give specific feedback on their performance and to help them set personal performance goals.

18. ____ I make sure there's an up-to-date training plan for both the whole team, as well as for each individual member.

19. ____ I routinely discuss our meetings with members then seek their ideas on how to improve them.

20. ____ About once a month I look over the empowerment chart for our team and actively seek ways of empowering people further.

21. ____ I don't necessarily run every meeting. I encourage others to take turns planning and running our meetings.

22. ____ I put a lot of emphasis on follow-through for all actions we've committed to implementing. I make sure we conduct regular monitoring activities to stay on track.

23. ____ I periodically engage the team in evaluating its effectiveness and taking corrective action.

24. ____ I'm an active sponsor of team initiatives. I go on their behalf to senior management, other teams and departments to get support and remove blocks.

25. ____ I make sure people get the credit they deserve for a job well done.

Leadership Self-Assessment Summary

Look over your ratings on the survey and ask:

1. What am I currently doing effectively as team leader?

2. What things do I need to learn or emphasize more?

3. What specific actions do I need to take to improve my performance as team leader?

Bibliography

Argyris, C. *Integrating the Individual and the Organization*. New York: Wiley, 1964.

Bennis, W. and others. *Essays in Interpersonal Dynamics*. Homewood, IL: Dorsey Press, 1979.

—. and Shepard H.A. "A Theory of Group Development." *Human Relations*, 1956.

Dyer, W.G. *Team Building: Issues and Alternatives*. Reading, MA: Addison Wesley, 1977.

Hackman, J. R. and Suttle, J.L. *Improving Life at Work*. Santa Monica, CA: Goodyear, 1977.

Lawler, E.E. *High Involvement Management*. San Francisco: Jossey-Bass, 1986.

Mintzberg, H. *The Nature of Managerial Work*. New York: Harper Row, 1977.

—. *Power in and Around Organizations*. Englewood Cliffs, NJ: Prentice Hall, 1983.

Ouchi, W.G. *Theory Z*. Reading, MA: Addison-Wesley, 1981.

Schein, E.H. *Organization Culture and Leadership*. San Francisco: Jossey-Bass, 1985.

—. "Improving Face-to-Face Relationships." *Sloan Management Review*, 1981.

—. and Bennis, W.G. *Personal and Organizational Change Through Group Methods*. New York: Wiley, 1965.

Senge, P., Kleiner A., Roberts, C., Ross, R., and Smith, B., *The Fifth Discipline Fieldbook*. New York: Double Day, 1994.

Srivastva, S. and associates. *The Executive Mind: New Insights on Managerial Thought and Action*. San Francisco: Jossey-Bass, 1983.

Tannenbaum, R. and Schmid, W. "How to Choose a Leadership Pattern." *Harvard Business Review*, 1958.

Tuckman, B.W. "Development Sequence in Small Groups." *Psychological Bulletin*, 1965.

—. and Jensen, M.A.C. "Stages of Small Group Development Revisited." *Group and Organizational Studies*, 1977.

Vroom, V.H. and Yetton, P.W. *Leadership and Decision Making*. Pittsburgh: University of Pittsburgh Press, 1973.

Understanding Interventions

*When a team shows signs of trouble,
this is your cue to step in and
make an intervention.
Here is the dictionary definition
of the word intervention:*

*Any action or set of actions, deliberately
taken to improve the functioning of an
individual, group, or organization.*

There are Two Types of Interventions: Immediate & Planned

Some interventions concern a specific incident that arises during the course of a meeting. This type of intervention has to be made immediately.

Some examples of situations calling for an *immediate* intervention:

- two people interrupting each other and not listening

- two people having a side conversation while a teammate is presenting their ideas

- one team member cutting another off in mid-sentence

- half the group going silent during a discussion

In these cases, members need to be stopped while the dysfunction is taking place and have their attention drawn to it so that it can be addressed on-the-spot with the corrective action. Immediate interventions can be sensitive, demanding the use of specific language and techniques. These are described in detail starting on page 36 of this chapter.

While the major focus of this manual is on making planned interventions, it's very important that every team leader develop excellent facilitation skills so that they can make effective immediate interventions.

This is especially critical whenever a team is storming. During this stage, leaders need to facilitate assertively and redirect the team away from ineffective behaviors before they become ingrained.

In addition to problems that need immediate attention, teams also encounter larger, on-going problems that call for planned interventions. These are situations that unfold over time and represent a pattern of behavior occurring within the team.

Examples of situations that require a *planned* intervention are:

- consistently poor follow-through on action plans

- on-going tension between two people on the team

- uneven workloads amongst members

- meetings that are poorly planned and unproductive

- lack of listening and mutual support for ideas presented at team meetings

In contrast to the fast, in and out nature of immediate interventions, planned interventions are scheduled events. They require thorough planning and time set aside to conduct the actual intervention activities.

Choosing the Right Strategy When Your Team Needs Help

Whether you are making an immediate or planned intervention, there are two basic approaches to choose from: *heroic* or *facilitative*. Let's explore them each in-depth.

The Heroic Approach

This approach centers on the team leader or facilitator taking responsibility for fixing the team's problem. When a leader takes the heroic approach, he or she assesses the situation and decides who is right or wrong.

In an interpersonal conflict, the heroic approach might involve bringing the conflicting parties into the office for a talk, in which the leader strongly suggests what the parties ought to do. If the whole group is misbehaving, the heroic leader gives them a pep talk about teamwork. If there's a problem outside the team, he or she might go and negotiate on behalf of the team to settle a score.

One analogy for the heroic approach is to liken it to the role a parent plays with a group of immature children. But once a leader starts solving the team's problems, members know that any time there's a problem, they can run to the leader to have it solved for them.

The Facilitative Approach

This is a very different strategy in which the leader stays neutral and facilitates, while team members assess the team's situation and resolve it for themselves.

During interpersonal conflict a facilitative leader sizes up the situation only enough to choose the method or set of tools that the team members can use to solve their own problem. He or she then helps the members gather data about the situation to assess its meaning. Leaders who use the *facilitative* approach set the stage so that members are enabled to give each other feedback, seek solutions and create action plans. At the end of a facilitated intervention, members are responsible for implementing improvements.

The analogy for this approach is that of a coach. Next time the team has a problem they'll know that leader will be there to offer methods with which they can solve their own problems. They'll also know that they can't dump their problems onto the leader and expect them to be fixed.

You have probably sensed by now, that this manual is strongly biased towards the facilitative approach. It's important that you understand this, since all of the interventions that are described on the pages ahead, will cast you in this neutral role. There are some very good reasons why we encourage you to use the facilitative approach :

- If the leader always fixes their problems, team members will stay in the dependent mode. This defeats the goal of all team leaders, which is to help their team mature to the performing stage.

- Any leader who takes all of the 'monkeys' onto his or her back, is soon overwhelmed with problems. Members become more accountable if they realize that team problems will be handed right back to them for resolution.

- Engaging members in solving their own problems is a powerful learning opportunity. Members get practice at giving and receiving feedback, dealing with conflict, handling emotions, and so forth. Whatever is learned from taking part in an intervention to resolve a sensitive situation is a thousand times more effective than any theoretical team building stuff taught in a workshop.

All leaders need to remember that the road to high performance leads through the territory called storming and that the only exit is through norming. Norming isn't about you solving the team's problems for the members:

> *True norming takes place when <u>members</u> solve their own problems and move forward with what they've learned.*

The Challenge of Facilitating Interventions

While the results of taking a facilitative approach are far superior to the outcomes of using the more directive, paternal approach, facilitating does present significant challenges:

- facilitating turns varying degrees of control over to the members, who might then proceed to come up with the wrong solution

- facilitating requires the use of tools and techniques that are still relatively unknown to most team leaders

- taking the facilitative approach takes extra time and seems a lot more complicated than just telling people what they ought to do

To help you overcome these challenges, we have described the steps you need to take to facilitate both immediate and planned interventions in very explicit detail in this manual. Once you've started to make facilitative rather than heroic interventions, it will become abundantly clear how giving team members an active role in solving their own problems puts overall team performance on fast forward.

Starting on page 40 you'll find an overview description of the six main techniques available for facilitating interventions. From page 145 onwards, we have also provided sample interventions for the twelve most common team troubles. By following the steps we have outlined, facilitating interventions should soon become second nature to both you and your team!

Before addressing planned interventions, lets first look at the key skills and techniques for making immediate interventions.

Facilitating Immediate Interventions

Imagine that you're in a team meeting. The discussion has been going in circles for the past hour. Two people are emotionally repeating their views of the situation without listening to each other. The rest of the team sits in silence. Two other members are holding a side conversation and three others are busy writing.

If your team starts to exhibit these or other inappropriate behaviors and you do nothing about them, your meetings will soon deteriorate and you'll be seen as a weak and ineffective leader!

To help you avoid simply correcting the members, in the heroic manner, we offer the following steps that will let you facilitate an immediate intervention. These steps are:

1. Notice the dysfunction, don't ignore it.
2. Decide whether or not to intervene.
3. Stop the action.
4. Draw the attention of members to the symptoms.
5. Ask members to suggest an improvement or offer a suggestion for their consideration.
6. Implement the improvement.
7. Go back to the discussion.

Here's how that might look in the scenario described earlier:

1. You notice that people aren't paying attention and that the discussion is stalled.

2. Your assessment is that this is serious and should not be allowed to continue.

3. You say:

> *"I'd like to draw everyone's attention to the fact that only two people are actively engaged in this discussion while two others are side-chatting and the rest of you are writing."*

4. You ask:

> *"What can we do to get everyone back into the conversation and start making some progress?" They suggest improvements.*

5. You say:

> *"Let me sum up what you're suggesting. We take a 10 minute break, then reconvene to summarize the key points made so far, followed by going around the room to get each person's opinion on the best idea to implement."*

6. When people return from the break put their suggestions into action.

7. The meeting resumes.

Regardless of its length and complexity, an intervention is always an 'interruption'. You're stopping the group's discussion about the task and drawing member attention to the *process* or how the group is functioning. Since this interrupts the flow of discussion, the aim of the intervenor should always be to resolve the problem as quickly as possible, so that the team can return to its task.

Immediate Intervention Checklist

If you intervened every single time there was a problem, you would probably be interrupting your team too often. Instead you need to keep a watchful eye out for those situations where stepping in is necessary. Below is a mental checklist to use in deciding if an immediate intervention is advisable:

____ Is the problem serious?

____ Might it go away by itself?

____ How much time will it take to make the intervention? Do we have that time?

____ How much of a disruption will intervening cause?

____ How will it impact relationships?

____ How will it impact the flow of the meeting?

____ Can the intervention hurt the climate?

____ Will it damage anyone's self-esteem?

____ What's the chance the intervention will work vs. fail?

____ Do I know these people well enough to do this?

____ Do I have enough credibility to do this?

____ Is it appropriate given their level of openness and trust?

____ What will happen if I do nothing?

If your answers to the above questions support an intervention, then you're obligated to take action.

> *Failing to make an intervention, when one is truly needed, will cause the problem to deepen.*

The Structure of an Immediate Intervention

Once you have decided to make an immediate intervention, make sure you include the following statements:

Statement #1 - Awareness Statement

This draws the attention of the members to the problem situation by asking:

> *"I want to draw your attention to the fact that three people are writing and two others are engaged in a side conversation."*

Statement #1 is essential, since it gives the members the information they need in order to accept the need for an intervention.

Statement #2 - Impact Statement

This enables the members to understand the impact the current situation has created:

> *"As a result there are very few ideas on the board and we are far from the action plan we need to develop today."*

Statement #2 further builds the case for change. It tells the group about the impact of their current actions. Please note that this impact statement is often left out of interventions, especially if it has the potential to make the person or persons being talked to, feel guilty or embarrassed.

Statement #3 - Re-directing Statement

This statement tells members what to do:

> *"Lets all give this discussion our undivided attention."*

Rather than tell, this statement asks:

> *"What do you suggest we should do right now?"*

Statement #3 is the transition point. It either tells or asks for improvement. This part of the intervention is called the 'redirecting' statement since it spells out the behaviors that need to be implemented.

Telling Versus Asking

As already mentioned in the discussion about heroic versus facilitative interventions, you'll always be faced with the choice of either telling people what to do or asking for their suggestions. You'll need to make a judgment about which of these approaches to use, situation-by-situation. Below are some guidelines about whether to tell or ask.

- Asking is always better than telling because people are more likely to accept their own suggestions for improvement.

- Try asking first to see if the members offer a viable solution.

- Resort to telling people what to do if they're acting immaturely or don't offer any ideas.

- The more a group acts responsible and maturely, the more effective it is to ask and get them to collaborate on the intervention.

> *Remember... the best interventions are the ones you get the members to make themselves!*

Wording an Immediate Intervention

The rule that best describes how interventions should be worded is:

Say what you see.

As with any feedback, interventions should be descriptive and specific, not judgmental or attributive. The best course of action is to describe exactly what you see and avoid judging the situation. When you use descriptive rather than judgmental language, you protect people from losing esteem in front of others. The wording of an intervention should be like holding up a mirror to the participants so that they can see what they're doing and assess their dysfunction themselves.

To make sure your language is descriptive rather than judgmental look at the following examples:

Instead of...	Try...
"You seem bored."	"You've had your eyes closed for the last ten minutes."
"No one is paying attention."	"Three people are having a side conversation while I speak."
"Some people don't have opinions."	"We have only heard from Joe, Lisa, and Fred so far."
"This group is argumentative."	"You refuted Bill's idea before he had even finished."

Common Intervention Language

Since the wording of interventions is so important, here are some sentence stems or questions that are commonly used:

"I'm noticing that ..."

"I'd like to offer this observation ..."

"Let's stop for a moment and look at what's happening here ..."

"What are people experiencing right now?"

"How do people feel things have gone thus far?"

"A pattern I have observed is ..."

"I'd like to describe what I am seeing here and get your reaction to it ..."

In each of the above examples, the leader has set the stage for the members to notice their own situation.

Immediate Intervention Wording for Specific Situations

Below are some specific responses that can redirect ineffective behavior in different situations. You'll notice that none of these redirecting statements put the person down or is in anyway critical. All of them offer the other person a chance to recover and say, or do the right thing the next time.

You'll also notice that some responses include impact statements while others don't. In the examples where the facilitator is telling a member what to do, there's an underlying assumption that the member in question is unable or unwilling to make the appropriate corrective suggestion.

When people <u>run in and out</u> of a meeting, say:

> *"In the last ten minutes three people have gone in and out of this meeting disrupting the discussion. What should we do about this?"*

When everyone has <u>fallen silent</u>, say:

> *"Everyone has become pretty quiet in the last few minutes and we haven't had any new ideas. What can we do to get things going again?"*

When the whole group is acting <u>dysfunctional</u>, say:

> *"I'm going to stop this discussion. I'd like to describe what I'm noticing and get you to suggest what we can do to make the rest of this meeting run more smoothly."*

When members are <u>disregarding</u> their previously set group norms, say:

> *"I'm going to stop this meeting for a few minutes and ask you to look back at the norms set at the last meeting. Are we following them? Do we need to add a few new ones?"*

When the meeting has <u>totally digressed</u>, say:

> *"I need to point out that we've now digressed and are onto another topic. Is this the topic the team wants to discuss or should we park it and go back to the original agenda item?"*

When someone is being <u>sarcastic</u>, say:

> *"Ellen, I'm afraid your good ideas aren't being heard because of the tone of voice you're using. How about stating that again, only in a more neutral way?"*

When one person is <u>putting down</u> the ideas of another, say:

> *"Joe, you've been 'yah butting' every suggestion Carol has put on the table. I'm going to ask you to explore these ideas by asking a few questions to make sure you fully understand them before dismissing them. It'll make Carole feel more like she's being heard."*

When two people are <u>cutting each other off</u> and not listening to each other, say:

> *"I'm afraid neither of you are hearing the excellent points being made by the other. I'm going to ask you both to paraphrase what the other has said before making your own comment."*

When someone is <u>inappropriately aggressive</u> or hurtful to another person, say:

> *"Jason, I'm going to stop you from saying anything further for just a moment and ask Linda to tell you how she would like to have you interact with her during the rest of this meeting. Please listen to her without interrupting."*

When <u>one person dominates</u> the discussion, say:

> *"Al, you always have lots of valuable ideas, but we need to hear from the other members of the team. Would you please hold your comments until the end so that other people can be heard."*

When someone has hurled <u>a personal slur</u> at someone else, say:

> *"Jim, rather than characterizing Sally as being sloppy, please tell her specifically about the state of the meeting room after her session so that she can address the situation."*

When two people are <u>trashing each other's ideas</u> without giving them a fair hearing, say:

> *"You're discounting each other's ideas very quickly. I'm going to ask that you each give a quick snapshot of what the other person said, before launching into your own points."*

When a person just makes <u>negative remarks</u> about the ideas of another person, say:

> *"Mary, what do you like about what Chuck just said?"*

Making immediate interventions is an important leadership skill! In order to gain practice making immediate interventions, it's best to attend facilitation skills workshops that teach intervention skills.

Facilitating Planned Interventions

In contrast to immediate interventions, a *planned* intervention is required whenever there's an on-going team problem that needs to be solved.

Some examples of situations that call for planned interventions are:

- a team member who consistently fails to complete work on time

- two people who argue at meeting after meeting

- meetings that fail to achieve results week after week

- people who share their true feelings only outside of meetings

- poor communication within the team

- confusion about who is doing what

Unlike the fast in-and-out pace of an immediate intervention, planned interventions take time. All planned interventions demand both preparation and meeting time. It's our observation that they fall into six categories.

The Six Types of Planned Interventions

There are essentially six types of planned interventions depending on the situation. In each type, the intervenor is playing the facilitative or process role, while the members do the work of assessing the problem situation, developing solutions and making the needed changes. None of these interventions are heroic with the leader stepping in to dictate solutions.

The six types of facilitated, planned interventions are:

> **#1. Re-forming the team**
>
> **#2. Providing training**
>
> **#3. Identifying and solving team problems**
>
> **#4. Sharing feedback**
>
> **#5. Coaching individual members**
>
> **#6. Mediating conflicts**

It's important to note that other than the last two categories, coaching of individual members and conflict mediation, the other four techniques are conducted with the full participation of the whole team. That means that in four of the intervention types, the team's problems are not taken off-line and dealt with behind closed doors, but are dealt with out in the open, with team members actively participating.

Experienced managers and supervisors will be most familiar with problem resolution strategies that take the problem off-line. While this may work when a problem is confined to one or two individuals, it's not an effective way of resolving problems that involve a group.

While there's a certain danger in laying a problem on the table for all to see, it's a necessary step when the problem is being experienced by the whole team. In these situations it's important that all of the members be involved in working things out, in order to get true commitment to the resolution.

While these participatory techniques are known to be effective, they're understandably intimidating for leaders who haven't used them before. Without structure and proper planning, even a well intentioned discussion of any sensitive issue has the potential to make that situation worse! In other words, planned interventions can go wrong and, therefore, need to be carefully structured and even more carefully implemented.

Fortunately there are tested methods that remove some of the risk in making interventions and ensure success. On the following pages you'll find an outline of each intervention type, their main process steps and associated tools.

Planned Intervention Type #1. Re-forming the Team

Situation

When a team is first formed, it needs to go through a structured team formation activity in order to get off to a solid start. If a team is launched in an ad hoc manner and starts operating without a clear framework, confusion inevitably results. In these cases the team needs to go back to the beginning and hold a comprehensive launch discussion. This is especially true if:

- a clear team 'goal statement' is missing

- there's a lack of specific objectives and/or detailed work plans

- the team is operating without a set of rules or norms

- roles and responsibilities are poorly defined

- there's no skills profile or training plan

- the team lacks a communications plan

Symptoms

Teams that need re-forming usually exhibit considerable confusion about where they're going. Members may be pulling in different directions or pursuing their personal goals instead of the team's goals. There may also be a lack of progress towards achieving group goals and the associated results. People outside of a poorly defined team are usually confused about what that team does or how to relate to it.

Intervention Process

Conducting an intervention to re-form a team that was incompletely launched in the first place consists of the following steps:

1. The team's situation is diagnosed by conducting individual interviews with members.

2. If people are reluctant to divulge information or if anonymous data is desired, a survey can be conducted.

3. Survey data is then tabulated and fed back to the members.

4. A team formation workshop is planned so that the members can develop the missing pieces of their team's structure.

5. Follow-up is scheduled to ensure all of the team formation elements are in place.

Steps in a Team Launch

Any team in this situation needs to set aside time to establish a clear framework for its operation. This can be done all at once, during a one or two-day team formation workshop, or integrating the team formation activities into several consecutive meetings.

Whatever format is chosen, the team formation process ensures all members achieve clarity in the following ten areas:

1. **Familiarity** - members need to get to know each other in order to build relationships and create a comfortable and trusting environment.

2. **Team Goal** - there needs to be a clear team goal that's created by the members.

3. **Skills Profile** - members need to know each other's strengths and learning goals in order to be able to create effective work plans that exploit member talents.

4. **Norms** - all teams need a set of team rules, created by the members, by which they agree to govern themselves.

5. **Decision-making** - teams need orientation to the main decision-making options and agree as to when and how to use each approach.

6. **Customers, Products and Services Profile** - every team needs to be clear about who they're serving and which products and services they're providing.

7. **Work Objectives and Results Indicators** - teams need to ensure that there are specific objectives and detailed action plans in place to achieve the team's goal.

8. **Empowerment Plans** - teams need to understand clearly which types of decisions they're allowed to make and to what extent they're empowered to implement changes.

9. **Roles and Responsibilities** - the members of any team need to understand who'll do what and how their roles are connected to each other.

10. **Communication Plan** - each team needs to establish a clear plan that describes who'll be informed about the team's activities and what form that contact will take.

Once a team has completed its formation discussions, it can create a summary called a *Team Charter*. The Team Charter document can then be circulated throughout the organization to let others know about the role of the team.

To determine whether or not your team needs to undergo a full or partial re-formation activity, use the following diagnostic instrument.

Team Formation Survey

In order to determine if your team needs to hold discussions aimed at establishing a clear framework to guide its operations, would you please respond to the following questions. Remember that this survey is anonymous.

1. *Familiarity:* How well do you know the other members of this team? Have you been properly introduced to them? Do you know their personal goals, likes, dislikes, talents and interests?

1	2	3	4	5
Don't know the others		Know some things about a few people		Know others quite well

2. *Goal clarity:* How clear are you about the overall goal of the team?

1	2	3	4	5
Unsure of our goal		Somewhat sure about our goal		Clear about our goal

3. *Member profile:* How clear are you about other member's individual skills? To what extent do you know who is an expert in specific areas?

1	2	3	4	5
Don't know members' skills		Know the skills of some members		Clear about skills of all members

4. *Rules:* Does the team have a set of team rules or norms that members use to govern relations and meeting management? Does the team use and update its rules from time to time?

1	2	3	4	5
We have no rules		We have rules but don't use them		We post our rules and use them

5. **Decision-making options:** Has the team explored the different decision-making options and does the team consciously select the method best suited to each situation?

1	2	3	4	5
We are not aware of the decision options		Sometimes consider how we will make a decision		We are always conscious about how we make decisions

6. **Customers, products and services:** Has the team created a profile of who its customers are and what products and services it provides?

1	2	3	4	5
No profile exists		We are somewhat clear about the profile		We have a profile

7. **Work objectives and results measures:** Does the team have detailed objectives that include specific results indicators that describe how the team plans to achieve its goal?

1	2	3	4	5
We don't have either		We have some objectives and/or some measures		We have both

8. **Empowerment plan:** Does the team have a clear picture of which decisions it can make and which require management approval?

1	2	3	4	5
There is no empowerment plan		We are clear about some items		We are clear about how empowered we are

9. **Roles and responsibilities:** Are you clear about what's expected of you and how your role relates to the roles of other team members?

1	2	3	4	5
I'm unclear		I'm somewhat clear		I'm totally clear

10. **Communication plan:** Does the team have a plan that describes who it should communicate with, when, and how?

1	2	3	4	5
No plans		Somewhat planned		We have a plan

Comments:

Return the completed survey to:

(Name/Address/Fax or e-mail)

Planned Intervention Type #2. Providing Training

Situation

The team is pulled together and starts to meet. Because of time and workload pressures, no time is set aside for training. There's an assumption that people are skilled at running meetings, making group decisions, and that being on a team isn't any different than being in a regular work group. The leader receives no training either and carries on chairing team meetings pretty much like he or she ran departmental meetings in the past.

Symptoms

There are a variety of signals that tell you a team is in need of a training intervention. These can include: poorly run meetings, ineffective decision-making, conflicts that go unattended, inability to keep discussions on-track, rude or inappropriate interpersonal behaviors, dominance by a few members, an autocratic leadership style, lack of processes to manage complex group discussions, lack of facilitation and/or poor work planning and execution. On top of these team-related training needs, most teams also need periodic training in their technical field and in administrative skills such as budgeting, the use of computers, etc.

Intervention Process

All good training is implemented using the following steps:

1. A needs assessment is conducted to determine exactly which skills members most need to acquire. In addition to a written assessment, the person planning the training is well advised to attend at least one team meeting as an observer. This allows for first hand observation of the team's internal processes and how members interact.

2. Once learning needs have been assessed, specific training modules can be designed.

3. The training is implemented.

4. A follow-up evaluation is conducted to determine the effectiveness of the training intervention.

Depending on the time and money available, training can take the form of full or half-day training workshops, mini-training bursts interjected into staff meetings, the use of training videos and/or providing members with books or articles to read. Since few teams have extra time to devote to training, a creative mixture of activities is often required.

The skills that teams need fall into a number of distinct categories. These include technical skills related to the team's task, administrative skills such as budgeting, plus those skills that relate specifically to being an effective team such as interpersonal, meeting, and facilitation skills.

Since we can't anticipate your team's technical training needs here, we're focusing on the teaming and interpersonal skills that every team needs in order to function effectively. You can use the following *Team Skills Needs Assessment* and the *Training Intervention Planning Worksheet* (page 49) if you suspect that your team is in trouble because they lack training in team-related skills.

 ## Team Skills Needs Assessment

Look over the following skill areas and put a number beside each item using the following scale:

1 = Don't know?

2 = I have no background with this particular item and would like to learn more

3 = I have some background in this area but would still like to learn more

4 = I have had enough training in this area to feel that I am at a satisfactory level

5 = I have had enough training and/or experience in this area to feel confident about my skills

6 = I am skilled enough in this area to teach it to others or act as a resource to the team

<u>**Team Concept**</u>   <u>**Your Ranking**</u>

Understanding of the team concept and the basic principles
of how teams work   _____

Understanding of how teams are different from regular
work groups   _____

Awareness of the stages of team development particularly
the potential for storming   _____

Understanding of team empowerment   _____

Clarity about the role of each team member
and what is expected of us   _____

Clarity about the role of the team leader and
the relationship with team members   _____

Clarity about the parameters and processes that
relate to the operation of this team   _____

Meeting Skills

Understanding of the components of a good team meeting   _____

Understanding of the role of a meeting chairperson   _____

Knowledge of how to structure an agenda   _____

Knowledge of how to manage time and control
the flow of discussions   _____

Awareness of decision-making options and
how to use them to make good decisions   _____

Knowledge of how to keep accurate minutes   _____

Facilitation Skills

Awareness of the concept and role of a facilitator   _____

Knowledge of when to use facilitation instead of chairing _____

Familiarity with the key tools and techniques of facilitation _____

Knowledge of techniques to get full member participation _____

Skill in managing group conflicts   _____

Ability to use the most common quality/process improvement
tools and techniques   _____

Personal and Interpersonal Skills

Awareness of the behaviors and roles that make members effective   _____

Awareness of the behaviors and roles that make members
ineffective   _____

Knowledge of the techniques for giving and receiving feedback   _____

Skill at managing my own emotions   _____

Understanding of the difference between debating and arguing   _____

Skill at listening to and supporting the ideas of others   _____

Ability to work cooperatively with others to achieve team goals   _____

Ability to communicate my ideas verbally and in writing   _____

Skill and comfort at making presentations   _____

Knowledge of project planning and management tools
and techniques   _____

Skill at managing my own time and workload so that commitments   _____
are met

Other knowledge or skills I feel I need to become more effective:

_____

_____

_____

_____

_____

_____

_____

_____

_____

_____

Training Intervention Planning Worksheet

Tabulate and then review the *Team Skills Needs Assessment.*

Which areas received the highest ratings as an indicator of skills most people already possess?

_____

_____

_____

Which areas received the lowest ratings as an indicator of the skills that members most need to acquire?

_____

_____

_____

How can these training needs best be met?

_____ formal training session held for the entire team

_____ individuals sent to specialized training

_____ just-in-time training held during a regular team meeting

_____ giving members books to read

_____ showing videos

_____ providing practice and feedback sessions

_____ coaching selected individuals

other: _____

_____

_____

Planned Intervention Type #3.
Identifying & Solving Team Problems

Situation

When any team experiences problems that aren't confined to one individual, aren't based on a lack of skills and/or aren't behavioral in nature, there's usually an 'issue' that needs to be identified and resolved. These problems can be from within the team, but can also come from outside.

Symptoms

Some examples of situations that represent problems a team needs to solve include: late deadlines for orders, lack of adequate equipment, insufficient computer capacity and uneven workloads, to mention only a few.

Intervention Process

When a team has a problem to solve, use the steps of the *Systematic Problem-Solving Model*, (pages 52-57) which are:

1. Name the problem by gathering data to make sure members understand the problem area. If the problem isn't readily apparent it may be useful to use a tool like *Forcefield Analysis* (page 51) to sort and then prioritize issues that need to be resolved. Once a clear problem has been identified, facilitate a discussion to generate a one or two-sentence statement of the problem.

2. Set a goal for the problem-solving exercise so that the members of the team are aligned about the desired outcome.

3. Conduct a thorough analysis of the facts surrounding the problem so that everyone has a clear and shared understanding of the current situation. Make sure you look beyond symptoms to causes.

4. Generate ideas that solve the problem. Use a technique such as brainstorming to generate as many ideas as possible.

5. Evaluate the ideas by creating *criteria* for sorting the good ideas from those that are less useful. Use the criteria to identify the best options for improving the problem situation.

6. Create detailed action plans to ensure that everyone is clear about what will be done, how, by whom, and by when. Identify how and when action plans will be implemented.

The *Systematic Problem-Solving* worksheets on the following pages are useful to help guide members through their discussions.

Identifying the Problem

Before you attempt to problem-solve, the team may need to go through a problem identification process.

This could involve holding interviews or conducting a survey to gather opinions and input from whoever is involved in the problem situation. The target audience could be customers, suppliers, management or the members of another team. Identifying problems could also involve mapping out a current process to find out what's working and what's not.

The tool known as *Forcefield Analysis* is outlined below as it might be used if the team were experiencing a problem. This tool is very useful as a means of facilitating a total group discussion on possible underlying causes of the problem facing the team, and for prioritizing the causes. An example of the use of this tool is located at the top of the next page.

Conducting a Forcefield Analysis

Step 1. Identify the issue and the goal of the problem-solving exercise.

Step 2. Divide a flipchart sheet in half. On the left side facilitate a discussion amongst members to answer the question: *What's helping us? What are our strengths and resources?*

Step 3. On the right side facilitate a discussion about: *What's stopping us? What are our barriers?*

Step 4. Once both sides of the chart have been filled in, have the team prioritize the barriers that are stopping them. You can do this by giving each person three colored sticky dots for using on the flipchart to identify their choices as to the 1st, 2nd, and 3rd biggest barriers.

Step 5. Take the barrier that received the most votes and resolve it by facilitating the team using the problem-solving model on the next page. When each barrier has been removed, move on to the next priority item on the list.

Forcefield Analysis Example

Issue: The team is consistently unable to carry out the activities it plans, on schedule.			
Goal: To be able to implement 90% of our action plans on time.			

Forces for (what helps us?) ➡	⬅ Forces against (what stops us?)	Priority Vote
talent	daily fire-fighting of surprise issues	#2
commitment of members	people not trained to share roles	#1
new computers	computer scheduling capacity	#4
good meetings	meetings on wrong day of week	#3

Systematic Problem-Solving Worksheet #1

Step 1. Name the problem

Identify the problem that needs to be solved. Analyze it in just enough detail to create a common understanding. Use the space below to explore the general nature of the problem.

Now narrow in and select the specific aspect you wish to solve. Write a one or two-sentence problem statement to clearly define the problem.

Problem statement:

_____

_____

_____

_____

Systematic Problem-Solving Worksheet #2

Step 2. Identify the goal of the problem-solving exercise

Describe the desired outcome.

What would things look like if the problem disappeared? How would things look if this problem were resolved? Use the space below to record the ideas generated.

Now narrow in and write a one or two-sentence goal statement.

Goal statement:

_____

_____

_____

_____

Systematic Problem-Solving Worksheet #3

Step 3. Analyze the problem

Dissect the problem thoroughly. Avoid coming up with solutions. Instead, concentrate on making sure that everyone is clear about the specific nature of the situation. Don't focus on symptoms, but delve behind each effect to determine the root causes.

Use an analysis tool such as 'Cause and Effect Charting' or a 'Fishbone Diagram' if the problem is a complex technical issue that has many contributing factors.

If you decide to use a simple questioning approach, ask:

- *How would we describe this problem to an outsider?*
- *What's taking place? What are the signs and symptoms?*
- *How are people affected? What makes this happen?*
- *What are the root causes of each symptom?*
- *What other problems does it cause?*
- *What are the most damaging aspects?*
- *What and who stops us from solving it?*
- *How do <u>we</u> contribute to the problem?*

Systematic Problem-Solving Worksheet #4

Step 4. Identify potential solutions

Use Brainstorming to generate a list of potential solutions to the problem.

If you use brainstorming, remember the rules:
  • let the ideas flow, be creative, don't judge
  • all ideas are accepted, even if they're way-out
  • build on the good ideas of others

Probing questions to ask once the group has run out of ideas:
  • *what if money were no object?*
  • *what if you owned this company?*
  • *what would the customer suggest?*
  • *what's the opposite of something already suggested?*
  • *what's the most innovative thing we could do?*

Record brainstorming ideas here:

Systematic Problem-Solving Worksheet #5

Step 5. Evaluate the solutions

Use the *Impact/Effort* Grid below to sift through the brainstormed ideas to determine which are best for the situation. Determine within your group what 'impact' and 'effort' mean for you. Eliminate any quadrant 4. solutions which have low impact and require a lot of effort.

		E f f o r t	
		Difficult To Do	*Easy To Do*
I m p a c t	*Major Improvement*	3.	1.
	Minor Improvement	4. ✗	2.

List all of the type 1 & 2 activities together for quick action	*List all of the type 3 activities here for development into action plans*

Systematic Problem-Solving Worksheet #6

Step 6. Plan for action

Create detailed action plans for items that need to be implemented. Make sure action plans adhere to a logical sequence of steps. Provide details about what will be done, how and by whom. Always put in target dates for completion. Identify the performance indicator that answers the question, *"How will we know we did a good job?"*

What will be done & how?	By whom?	When?	Performance Indicator

Planned Intervention Type #4. Sharing Feedback

Situation

When people work closely with each other on any team, there's a high need for cooperation and collaboration. This isn't always easy since each person has their individual work style which may clash with others. When people are upset with each other, or harbor concerns that go unexpressed, tensions rise and the stage is set for future conflict.

Symptoms

Members may be making snide remarks to each other, cliques may be forming, members may be shunning the team leader, the meetings may be constantly going off-track and trust levels may be at low levels.

Intervention Process

There are four areas around which all teams can and should regularly engage in feedback exercises. These four areas are *peer effectiveness, leadership effectiveness, meeting effectiveness, and team effectiveness.*

Peer Effectiveness

One way of diffusing tensions and allowing people to safely communicate what's bothering them and what they need from each other, is to implement a peer feedback session. Here's how it works:

1. Set aside at least twenty minutes at a team meeting for the feedback exercise.

2. Introduce the notion that feedback is an opportunity for personal team member growth and encourage each person to be open to accepting input from their peers. If you're the team leader, include yourself in the exercise.

3. Hand out the *Peer Feedback Worksheet*, a sample of which follows on the next page. Ask each person to put their name at the top of their sheet and then hand it to the person on their right.

4. As each sheet is passed around, ask each person to write at least one comment about the person whose name is at the top of the page in response to:

> *"What you do that is really effective? Keep doing it!"*
> *"What you could do to become even more effective."*

5. Sheets continued to be passed to the right until each person has written on all

of the sheets. Everyone gets their completed sheet back.

6. Each member is then asked to read the input confidentially and come to the next meeting ready to talk for two minutes about their personal plan to become more effective on the team. Again, remember to include yourself.

Because the feedback questions are both phrased in a positive manner and since the feedback isn't discussed openly, the danger of embarrassment is minimized. At the same time each person gets praise, plus specific tips about how they can improve.

Peer Feedback Worksheet

Write your name here: _____

What you do that's really effective and/or what you do that I really appreciate.

What you could do to become even more effective and/or what I need from you so that I can be more effective.

Leadership Effectiveness

In addition to peer feedback, every team needs a safe way of giving feedback to the leader. All effective team leaders know this and schedule a feedback exercise at least four times a year to surface and deal with relationship issues before they get large or damaging. Like the peer feedback process, this exercise also stresses positive actions that can make future relations better.

Intervention Process

There are essentially two ways to conduct this activity. The first is to anonymously implement the *Leadership Survey* on page 24. The tabulated results are given confidentially to the leader who then takes them to a coaching meeting with his or her manager. The leader also reports back to the team on what the survey indicated to be their strengths, as well as describing what actions he or she will be taking in order to improve.

At minimum, the leadership survey should be implemented twice a year as a preventative measure, or used as part of any intervention into a problem situation involving the leader.

The second method of implementing leadership feedback is to hold what is known as a *Needs and Offers* exercise. This often isn't as comprehensive as a leadership survey, but has the advantage of being a face-to-face exercise. To conduct a *Needs and Offers* exercise, use the following steps:

1. Introduce the exercise as a really positive and safe means of giving each other feedback.

2. The leader leaves the room and the team chooses a facilitator. Together the members answer two questions:

> i. *What we need from you as our leader?*
> ii. *What we're offering you in return?*

3. In another room, the leader jots down his/her answers to similar questions:

> i. *What I need from you to be able to lead effectively?*
> ii. *What I'm offering you in return?*

4. The leader then returns and the group presents what it needs. The leader listens and asks clarifying questions only. He or she then reads their needs.

5. The team members then read out what they're offering the leader in return.

Again the leader listens and asks clarifying questions only, then finally reads his or her offers.

6. The facilitator then leads a discussion of the main points covered. The activity ends when both parties agree on the actions they will mutually implement.

This *Needs and Offers* exercise doesn't name faults or lay blame. Because it's forward looking, it very constructively creates a safe forum in which each side can ask the other for what it needs.

Team Effectiveness

One approach to conducting a team tune-up, when there are problems, is to implement a survey that asks a broad and fairly comprehensive range of questions about the team. These questions can cover everything from *trust* and *goal clarity*, to the current status of *interpersonal relations*.

Implementing a team effectiveness survey consists of creating a survey instrument that asks the questions that are relevant to the team. This survey is then completed anonymously and returned to a neutral third party to tabulate. Time is set aside at a meeting to review the raw data and identify those things that got low ratings.

These problems are then prioritized using a form of *multi-voting*. The top priority issues are then problem-solved using the *Systematic Problem-Solving Model* previously described, starting on page 52.

While it's always best to create your own survey, a generic sample is provided on page 63.

A second less formal way of identifying areas for team improvement is to look over a list of the characteristics of a high performance team (page 1) and then compare your team to those criteria. As the facilitator you must ask members two questions in the following sequence:

> *"In what ways are we behaving like a high performance team?"*
> *"In what ways are we <u>not</u> behaving like a high performance team?"*

Both positives and negatives are recorded on a flipchart using two columns as in the following example. For each item in the negative column, possible solutions and prescriptions are identified.

Areas of Effectiveness	Areas of Ineffectiveness	Prescriptions
high trust levels	workload is uneven	hold work planning session
great meetings	a few people dominate	Round-robin to get ideas

Meeting Effectiveness

A team is only as good as its meetings, so they need to be monitored and tuned-up on a regular basis. Of the many techniques for getting feedback about meetings, we recommend the following two approaches:

Approach #1 – Formal Survey

On a more formal note we recommend that every team have a *Meeting Effectiveness Survey* that is implemented at least twice each year. The process for this is exactly the same as for the *Team Effectiveness Survey*. Again we recommend that you create your own instrument, but have provided a generic sample on page 66.

Approach #2 – Exit Surveys

The second technique we recommend for all teams is more informal and can be used more frequently; for exmample, at the end of every team meeting. This method is known as an *Exit Survey*. Here's how to use one:

1. On a single flipchart sheet, write up to five questions about the team's meetings. The questions you ask will depend on the elements the team is having most problems with. It could be openness, sharing, the pace of the meeting, the quality of decisions or how well the team stays on-topic.

2. Post this sheet right beside the main exit door, and ask each person to quickly rate each item as they leave.

3. At the start of the next meeting, bring out the survey sheet and ask members to interpret the results. Ask them specifically what the team can do at today's meeting to improve any low ratings. Write down and implement any suggestions agreed to by the group.

4. Keep implementing the surveys using the same specific elements until they start to get high ratings, then change the questions to probe in other areas.

A sample *Exit Survey* is provided on page 69.

Team Effectiveness Survey

Instructions: Please give your candid opinion of this team by rating its characteristics on the seven-point scale shown below. Circle the appropriate number on each scale to represent your evaluation. Remain anonymous. Return the survey in the envelope provided. The results will be discussed with the whole team. *Remember, you're rating your immediate work team.*

1. Goal Clarity
Are goals and objectives clearly understood and accepted by all members?

1	2	3	4	5	6	7

Goals and objectives aren't known,
understood, or accepted

Goals are clear
and accepted

2. Participation

Is everyone involved and heard during group discussions, or is there a "tyranny of a minority"?

1	2	3	4	5	6	7

A few people tend
to dominate

Everyone is active
and has a say

3. Consultation
Are team members consulted on matters concerning them?

1	2	3	4	5	6	7

We are seldom
consulted

Team members are
always consulted

4. Decision-making
Is the group both objective and effective at making decisions?

1	2	3	4	5	6	7

The team is ineffective
at reaching decisions

The team is very effective
at reaching decisions

5. Roles and Responsibilities
When action is planned, are clear assignments made and accepted?

1	2	3	4	5	6	7

Roles are poorly
defined

Roles are clearly and
fairly defined

6. Procedures

Does the team have clear rules, methods and procedures to guide it? Are there agreed to methods for problem-solving?

1	2	3	4	5	6	7

There is little structure, and we lack procedures

The team has clear rules and procedures

7. Communications

Are communications between members open and honest? Do members listen actively?

1	2	3	4	5	6	7

Communications are not open, not enough listening

Communications are open. People listen

8. Confronting Difficulties

Are difficult or uncomfortable issues openly worked through or are conflicts avoided? Are conflicts worked through?

1	2	3	4	5	6	7

Difficulties are avoided or there's little direct conflict management

Problems are attacked openly and directly

9. Openness and Trust

Are team members open in their transactions? Are there hidden agendas? Do members feel free to be candid?

1	2	3	4	5	6	7

Individuals are guarded and hide their motives

Everyone is open and speaks freely

10. Commitment

How committed are team members to deadlines, meetings, and other team activities?

1	2	3	4	5	6	7

Deadlines and commitments are often missed

Total commitment

11. Support

Do members pull for each other? What happens when one person makes a mistake? Do members help each other?

1	2	3	4	5	6	7

Little evidence of support

Lots of support

12. Risk-taking

Do individuals feel they can try new things, risk failure? Does the team encourage risk?

1	2	3	4	5	6	7

Little support for risk

Lots of support for risk

13. Atmosphere

Is the team atmosphere informal, comfortable, and relaxed?

1	2	3	4	5	6	7

The team spirit is tense

The team is comfortable and relaxed

14. Leadership

Are leadership roles shared or do the same people dominate or control?

1	2	3	4	5	6	7

A few people dominate

Leadership is evenly shared

15. Evaluation

Does the team routinely stop and evaluate how it's doing in order to improve?

1	2	3	4	5	6	7

We never evaluate

We routinely evaluate

16. Meetings

Are meetings orderly, well-planned, and productive?

1	2	3	4	5	6	7

Waste of time

They couldn't be better

17. Fun

Is there an "esprit de corps" or sense of fun on this team?

1	2	3	4	5	6	7

Humbug!

We have fun

Meeting Effectiveness Survey

Instructions: Please give your candid opinions of the meetings you attended as part of this group. Rate the characteristics of the meetings by circling the appropriate number on each scale to represent your evaluation. Remain anonymous. Return the survey to your group facilitator. *Remember, you are rating the meetings of this group.*

I. MEETING OBJECTIVES

Are objectives clearly set out in advance of the meeting?

I	2	3	4	5	6	7

Objectives are seldom
set out in advance

Objectives are always
set out in advance

2. COMMUNICATION

Are agendas circulated to all members in advance of the meeting?

I	2	3	4	5	6	7

Agendas are rarely
circulated in advance

Agendas are always
circulated in advance

3. START TIMES

Do meetings start on time?

I	2	3	4	5	6	7

Meetings hardly ever
start on time

Meetings always start
on time

4. TIME LIMITS

Are time limits set for each agenda item?

I	2	3	4	5	6	7

We do not set
time limits

Time limits are always
set for each item

5. MEETING REVIEW

Are action items from the previous meeting(s) brought forward?

I	2	3	4	5	6	7

Items are seldom
brought forward

Items are always brought
forward from previous meetings

6. WARM-UP

Is there a meeting warm-up to hear from all members?

I	2	3	4	5	6	7

We seldom use
a meeting warm-up

We often use a
meeting warmup

7. ROLE CLARITY

Are roles (i.e., timekeeper, scribe, facilitator) made clear?

1	2	3	4	5	6	7

Roles are not
identified

Roles are always
clearly defined

8. SETTING

Is there a quiet place for the meeting, with ample work space, flipcharts, and AV support?

1	2	3	4	5	6	7

The meeting place is
not well suited

The meeting place
is very good

9. PROCESS

Is there clarity before each topic as to how that item will be managed?

1	2	3	4	5	6	7

There is rarely any
planning on processon process

There is always clarity

10. PREPARATION

Does everyone come prepared and ready to make decisions?

1	2	3	4	5	6	7

We are often
unprepared

We are generally
prepared

11. INTERRUPTIONS

Are meetings being disrupted due to people leaving, phones ringing, pagers beeping, etc.

1	2	3	4	5	6	7

There are constant
interruptions

We control
interruptions

12. PARTICIPATION

Are all members fully exchanging views, taking responsibility for action items and follow-up?

1	2	3	4	5	6	7

People hold back and
don't take ownership

Everyone offers ideas
and takes action

13. LEADERSHIP

Does one person make all the decisions, or is there a sharing of authority?

1	2	3	4	5	6	7

The manager holds the chair
and makes most decisions

Authority is shared

14. PACE

How would you rate the pace of the meetings?

1	2	3	4	5	6	7

Poor   Just right

15. TRACKING

Do meetings stay on-track and follow the agenda?

1	2	3	4	5	6	7

Meetings usually stray off track   Meetings usually stay on track

16. RECORD KEEPING

Are quality minutes kept and circulated?

1	2	3	4	5	6	7

Yes, they are   No, they are not

17. LISTENING

Do members practice active listening?

1	2	3	4	5	6	7

We don't listen closely to each other   Members listen actively

18. CONFLICT MANAGEMENT

Are differences of opinion suppressed, or is conflict effectively used?

1	2	3	4	5	6	7

Conflict isn't very effectively used   Conflict is effectively exploited for new ideas

19. DECISION-MAKING

Does the group generally make good decisions at our meetings?

1	2	3	4	5	6	7

We tend to make poor decisions   We tend to make good decisions

20. CLOSURE

Do we tend to end topics before getting into new ones?

1	2	3	4	5	6	7

We constantly start new topics   We close each topic before moving on

21. CONSENSUS

Do we work hard to make collaborative decisions that we can all live with?

1	2	3	4	5	6	7

We abandon consensus
too easily

We work hard
to reach consensus

22. FOLLOW-UP

Is there good coherent follow-up to commitments made at meetings?

1	2	3	4	5	6	7

We tend not to
follow-up

There is consistent
follow-up

Exit Survey

Give us your assessment of the items below.

1. OUTPUT: How well did we achieve what we needed to?

1	2	3	4	5
Poor	Fair	Satisfactory	Good	Excellent

2. USE OF TIME: How well did we use our time?

1	2	3	4	5
Poor	Fair	Satisfactory	Good	Excellent

3. PARTICIPATION: How well did we do on making sure everyone was involved equally?

1	2	3	4	5
Poor	Fair	Satisfactory	Good	Excellent

4. DECISION-MAKING: How well thought out were our decisions?

1	2	3	4	5
Poor	Fair	Satisfactory	Good	Excellent

5. ACTION PLANS: How clear and doable are our action plans?

1	2	3	4	5
Poor	Fair	Satisfactory	Good	Excellent

Planned Intervention Type #5. Coaching Individual Members

Situation

While most team problems need to be dealt with by the whole team, there are situations when the whole team's effectiveness is being hampered by the actions or behavior of one member. The person who is the source of the problem may be unaware of the impact of their actions or they may simply lack the skills needed to fulfill job requirements.

Symptoms

The same team member consistently fails to meet deadlines, doesn't carry his or her share of the workload, or acts inappropriately at meetings. The inappropriate behavior may be rudeness, engaging in conflict, constantly criticizing other people's ideas, or using attention getting tactics. Members who engage in poor behavior or fail to do their work are often shunned by other members. The other members of the team may come to you after meetings to complain and demand that you do something about that person.

Intervention Process

When one individual is performing poorly or is acting out, taking them aside for personal coaching may be the right thing to do. While this person most likely also needs to receive personal feedback from peers (see *Planned Intervention Type #4*, page 58), personal coaching works best if the member is having a personal performance problem which would be too embarrassing to put on the table for the whole team to discuss or which is based in personal problems or work habits.

Dealing with a problem team member in privacy offers them the opportunity to change their ways before their actions become the focus of an activity involving the whole team.

As with all other interventions, the purpose of a coaching intervention is to help, not to punish. The coaching intervention process includes offering feedback, making the underperformer aware of the impacts of their actions and then supporting him/her in finding and implementing solutions. This is achieved by getting the problem performer to make their own assessment, help them come up with improvement suggestions and ensure that they take responsibility for making changes.

In any coaching intervention the team leader has to avoid the temptation of being *directive* by telling the person what to do, especially as the first course of action.

Facilitating, rather than directing, makes the other person assume responsibility for their actions and their personal change plan.

When an individual team member requires one-on-one coaching from the team leader, the following steps are suggested:

Steps in the Coaching Process

1. Keep detailed notes on the specifics of the team member's performance problem. This means keeping track of what they do, how often they do it and the impact their poor performance has. This information is needed in order to offer specific performance feedback.

2. Ask the other person to identify a convenient time for a meeting. Tell them exactly what it's about. Find a private place for the meeting.

3. Write the specific, detailed feedback about their performance on either a flipchart or a sheet of paper. This lets you refer to your notes and also provides the member with written notes at the end of the session.

4. Set a clear context for the session. Start by thanking them for coming and explain that your purpose is to offer feedback about their performance so that they can improve. Explain your approach as being confidential, supportive, and in partnership with them. Let them know that your approach will consist of giving specific feedback and then helping them seek improvements. Be clear about the outcome you expect: that they will leave with clear plans for personal improvement.

5. Identify the general area of concern and ask them to give you their perception of how they're performing. Listen actively to determine their level of self-awareness and openness to change. Paraphrase their key points.

6. Express empathy about how hard it is to receive feedback, but ask them to listen to you without interrupting or getting defensive while you present your data to them. Ask the member not to interrupt or contradict you, but do invite him/her to ask questions for clarification purposes.

7. Share your feedback in a totally factual, specific manner. Don't attribute motives or label the other person. Keep it objective, saying for example:

> *"For the last three weeks you have not completed your team commitments on time."*

Saying "*your work is always late*" is too general and attributes negative characteristics to the person. Answer all specific questions they may have.

8. For each feedback point also let the person know about the impact of their actions on others. Again be very specific, for example:

> *"When you failed to get the budget information to Mary, she had to gather the data herself and work six hours overtime to make the budget deadline."*

9. Objectively review the facts of the situation, incorporating whatever information you obtained from hearing the team member's version of the situation. Then ask him or her to identify solutions.

10. Be very supportive of any suggestions made by the team member, since the most effective ideas are always those made by the person being coached. If, however, these suggestions aren't going to result in a significant improvement, describe the expected standard of performance in specific detail. For example:

> *"The team needs you to take action on all of the items you commit to at team meetings. When commitments can't be completed on time, you need to contact affected members as soon as possible."*

Answer any questions that the member might have about the standard. Be open to making any reasonable amendments.

11. Write down any action plans that have been discussed. Set clear time frames on this activity.

12. Offer any training and mentoring that might be needed.

13. Agree to a monitoring and report back mechanism. This could be in written form or in the form of another meeting between the two of you. Make sure they know exactly when and how you'll be following-up.

14. Compliment or otherwise reward the willingness of the team member to improve their performance.

This initial coaching event should be held to deal with a specific performance issue and viewed as a developmental process that's kept confidential. If the same problem persists, any subsequent meeting may need to go 'on the record' and be documented as part of the organization's performance management process.

Following you'll find a planning sheet to use when preparing to make a coaching intervention.

Coaching Intervention Planning Sheet

If you're about to conduct a coaching meeting with a team member, it's wise to plan what you're going to say to him or her in advance.

What will you say to set the proper, positive, context for the session? How are you going to say this? What words will work?

What will you say that shows appropriate empathy for his or her situation?

What specific feedback will you give him or her? How will you phrase this?

What specific impacts of their current performance will you make him or her aware of?

What are some of the options and solutions you'll propose?

What are some of the support mechanisms you plan to offer?

What can you say to end on a positive note?

Coaching Intervention Checklist

Use the following checklist to monitor your own performance in making a coaching intervention. Did you:

_____ base the session on observable, specific, factual information about the person's performance

_____ keep it non-personal

_____ show understanding

_____ use good active listening techniques

_____ frame it as a developmental, non-punitive meeting

_____ remain optimistic

_____ communicate the problem very clearly

_____ identify the negative impacts of the current situation

_____ set forth clear expectations

_____ act appropriately assertive

_____ ensure the team member feels ownership for improvements

_____ offer suggestions when the member is clearly stuck

_____ take a problem-solving approach

_____ makes sure there are clear next steps

_____ plan for follow-up with the team member

_____ offer congratulations and appropriate recognition for any improvements that are made

Planned Intervention Type #6. Mediating Conflicts

Situation

One of the realities of teams is that two or more individuals on a team can get locked into an intense interpersonal conflict that they can't resolve on their own. These situations become especially critical if hostility gets played out at team meetings. In these situations it's imperative that the conflict be settled quickly by making a timely intervention using third party conflict mediation techniques.

Symptoms

A conflict that needs mediation can involve two or more members of a team who are no longer on speaking terms and are locked in a personal battle with each other. They could be arguing about roles, territories, resources, or over a past incident that created a misunderstanding. Whatever the source, the parties are unable to settle their differences.

You know you need to intervene in a conflict if:
- a conflict between two people is out in the open and affecting others
- the conflict is getting emotional and personal
- peer feedback was tried but didn't resolve the situation
- the conflict is hurting either the team or its productivity
- members seem unwilling or unable to resolve the conflict themselves

Intervention Process

Like coaching, mediating a conflict between two people is an intervention type that needs to be made off-line. This is done to encourage openness and protect the privacy of the warring parties. The following description outlines how to conduct such an intervention. At the end of this description, you'll find a variation of this basic process for situations where the mediation involves two teams or two cliques on the same team.

1. Once you've determined that a mediation is needed, you need to approach each person separately and tell them that you'll be mediating the conflict that exists between them. Try to gain their consent, but don't hesitate to impose this process if they decline your offer. Resolving a festering conflict is not a voluntary activity.

2. Set a convenient time and find a very private place for the intervention.

3. When the parties arrive, seat them so they both face you. Ask them to not speak to one another.

4. You should have posted the rules for the session on a flipchart. Read these rules to the two individuals:

- each person will have a chance to present the facts of the case without interruption
- the other person will listen without comment
- no negative body language, negative comments or refuting of points are allowed
- anyone can ask for a break
- the session ends when everyone agrees that it's over
- the facilitator has the powers of a referee

5. Start with whoever wishes to go first, and let them tell their side of the conflict. Seat the parties face-to-face. The listener must make eye contact and periodically write down the key points made by the other person. He or she cannot argue back, however, they may ask probing questions for clarification purposes. The mediator should be writing down key points as well.

6. When the first speaker is done, ask the listener to report back a summary of what they thought they heard. This allows the speaker to correct for any misunderstandings or important missing information.

7. This process is then repeated with the second person speaking and the first speaker listening, making notes, then reading back their summary.

8. Once both parties have spoken, offer a neutral, third party summary of what you heard. Work with the two team members until they have created a conflict statement that they both agree represents the essence of their dispute. Write the summary statement on a flipchart.

9. Allow the two people to go away for as long as they need to think about what they've heard. During this time, they're to write down ideas/solutions that *they will enact themselves* to end the conflict.

10. When the mediation reconvenes, ask each person to share *at least three ideas* that describe what they need to do to resolve the conflict situation. Solutions should focus on self-improvement. This focus eliminates the temptation to place the blame and burden of change on the other person.

11. Facilitate a discussion to sort through the various suggestions to arrive at clear action plans. Your aim is to get each person to leave with a list of changes that they're

personally committed to making. Where appropriate, you can offer your assistance with things like training, coaching, etc.

12. Ensure that each person leaves with a written action plan. Make arrangements to touch base with each one in the next week or so.

13. Thank the two parties and congratulate them especially if they really made a sincere effort to settle their differences.

Interpersonal Conflict Mediation Summary Sheet

Mediating conflict between two people requires that you be an extremely assertive facilitator. You must be neutral at all times. You must also be very clear on the rules. Know the process you're going to use and spell it out — it's appropriate that the parties know that this is not a friendly chat. Conflict interventions are sensitive and difficult. Below is a summary of what's involved.

✓ Spell out the rules and the steps in the process.

✓ Be very assertive — make people stick to the rules.

✓ Stay in the neutral, facilitator role — this is their problem, not yours.

✓ Have them take turns speaking while the other person takes notes.

✓ Have them take turns summarizing back the other person's viewpoint.

✓ Make sure that each person has a clear and accurate understanding

   of the other person's main points.

✓ Make sure the key facts get written down on paper.

✓ Insist on strict confidentiality.

✓ Generate a summary of the key points in the conflict.

✓ Have participants identify the solutions they need to implement.

✓ Help participants write detailed and specific action plans.

✓ Thank them for participating.

✓ Plan to follow-up.

✓ Congratulate them on any progress made.

Mediating a Conflict Between Teams

When two teams get into conflict and start feuding over staff, resources or territory, a process very similar to the one used for solving interpersonal strife, can be used.

Intervention Process

When two teams are at war with each other, the best approach to resolving the differences between them consists of the following steps:

1. Find a neutral third party who isn't a member of either team, to be the facilitator for the mediation activities.

2. The facilitator speaks to both team leaders to get their buy-in and to explain the activity.

3. The facilitator then meets with each group separately to help them create a statement of their problem and the associated details of their situation.

4. At a joint meeting, the facilitator lays out the rules of the game and the proceedings start. Each team has a chance to present its version of the problem. The other team can only listen, ask clarifying questions, paraphrase key points and wrap up with a summary to indicate that the points made were understood. The teams then swap roles to allow the second team to present its version of the problem.

If the situation is fairly volatile:

5a. Separate the teams again and give them a chance to privately review what the other team said. Give them enough time to conduct a problem-solving exercise taking into consideration what they heard from the other team. Depending on the skills of each team, you may have to bring in facilitators for this exercise.

6a. Each team is then asked to come back to the table with viable solutions to the dilemma. These solutions can't be ones that ask the other team to make all the concessions or do all of the work. Each team has to give up some of what it wants in order to gain in other areas.

7a. When the two teams are together the facilitator allows each team to propose its solutions, then helps them to negotiate a compromise that removes the impasse.

If the situation isn't overly sensitive or volatile:

5b. The teams are kept together for a joint problem-solving session. Instead of looking for solutions alone, the two teams jointly identify the problem, set a goal, analyze the situation, and brainstorm solutions.

6b. At the end of the session, the members of the two teams jointly create action steps that resolve the conflict situation. Both parties must then commit to implementing their joint action plan.

Although the 'collaborative' problem-solving approach is the superior method for uniting the two teams (see 5b and 6b above), it unfortunately can't be applied in every situation. In those situations, when differences are too deep, a negotiated compromise may be the best outcome that can be achieved.

 Inter-Team Conflict Mediation Worksheet

In preparation for an inter-team mediation, determine the following:

What are the details of the conflict?

_____

_____

What have been the roles and attitudes of the team leader during this conflict?

_____

_____

How far apart are the two teams in terms of what they want?

_____

Totally dissimilar   50/50   Totally similar

What's been tried so far to settle the conflict? What were the results of those efforts?

_____

_____

How emotionally sensitive or volatile is the situation?

_____

Is the situation likely to be amenable to collaborative problem-solving, or will members need to be separated to come up with suggestions?

_____

_____

Combining Interventions to Meet Specific Needs

In the world of real teams, problems don't usually fall into just one of the six intervention categories described so far. In fact, most situations necessitate a blend of intervention techniques.

Here are just a few examples of interventions we've encountered in recent months. You'll note that each circumstance calls for its own blend of approaches.

Example #1

The team spent time forming, but still has poorly defined roles and responsibilities. In addition, three members are doing all the work, while the rest are doing very little.

Intervention Approach

Re-form the team to clarify roles and responsibilities. Then problem-solve the issue of uneven workloads and conduct a peer feedback exercise (Intervention Types #1, #3 & #4).

Example #2

The team exhibits poor meeting skills. People tend to argue and discussions go in circles. As a result of all the arguing, two members have now stopped speaking to each other. The team also has a bad track record of not following through on its action plans.

Intervention Approach

Members need a workshop on conflict management, effective group behaviors, meeting effectiveness and decision-making. The two combatants need to go through a mediation, facilitated by the leader or an outside party. Once members are trained they need to problem-solve the issues related to the lack of follow-through on action plans (Intervention Types #2, #3 & #6).

Example #3

The team's efforts are being hampered by the tight fisted rule of their autocratic leader. The roles and responsibilities of team members are unclear and there's a lot of debate about who's empowered to do what.

Intervention approach

The team leader needs to receive feedback from the members and may also need personal coaching from an external consultant or someone from H.R. Once the leader has started to let go, the team needs to re-form to clarify roles and responsibilities and establish a clear empowerment plan (Intervention Types #1, #4 & #5).

Starting on page 144, we provide you with 12 case studies that illustrate common intervention situations. These examples demonstrate just how unique and complex each situation is and reinforce the fact that most team problems need to be approached with a 'blend' of techniques.

Seeking Outside Help with an Intervention

You'll notice that in most of the situations we've described, the team leader is the person making the intervention.

> ***All team leaders need to know how to make both planned and immediate interventions.***

We believe that team leaders should make all interventions in their own team, unless:

- the situation is very sensitive and needs a neutral, third party
- the team leader doesn't have the experience needed to handle a complex or sensitive issue
- the issue to be discussed requires the input of all team members, including the team leader
- the problem is about the leader

In these instances, the team needs to turn to the Human Resources Department, the in-house trainer, the leader of another team, or an experienced external consultant.

Regardless of whether the team leader, an internal consultant or a paid professional makes an intervention, the steps and tools used are the same.

Are Interventions Optional?

All teams need to be told early in their life that team problems will always be surfaced and addressed. In other words, making an intervention when it's needed isn't optional. It's important that everyone know this because it's quite common for groups to back away from taking action, especially in tense interpersonal situations.

Even though the intervention itself isn't optional, there are many aspects of it that can and should be discussed with the group to gain their buy-in. These aspects include:

- the goal of the intervention
- its time and location
- the sequence of activities
- the conditions or rules that will be in effect during the activities

Getting the Authority to Make an Intervention

A common question team members ask is, *"Who has the authority to decide if an intervention is necessary?"* This is especially critical if the problem centers on the leadership style of the official team leader who isn't taking action to resolve the issues.

In an ideal world the organization that establishes teams should have a team implementation steering committee that oversees the management of the team concept. If this committee had planned thoroughly, they would have put in place a team maintenance schedule like the one proposed on page 135 in the section on *Prevention Strategies*. If the surveys and feedback exercises proposed in that section are followed, team problems will be surfaced and dealt with on a regular basis, before they become large. Any team based organization that hasn't implemented such a set of regular preventative activities is strongly advised to establish them immediately.

Since most interventions can be made by team leaders, it's important that they get intervention skills training so that they can spot the signs of trouble and take appropriate action. If team leaders aren't trained and no prevention mechanism exists, teams should at least be given a central facilitator, an H.R. person or Organization Development consultant with whom they can contact to request intervention assistance without recrimination.

The bottom-line is that making team interventions is a critically important aspect of team development that shouldn't be ignored!

A Note About Confidentiality

Whenever information is being gathered from team members, there needs to be an explicit guarantee given that all information will be treated confidentially. Without this assurance people can't be expected to share their true feelings. In any intervention this matter of confidentiality is somewhat tricky because the information being gathered also has to be fed back to the group as data.

To clear up any confusion, it's wise to be open about the following guidelines concerning the sharing of information:

- if any extremely sensitive, personal data is gathered, assurances must be given that it won't be revealed to the group

- all other information should be 'blended' together with other responses to create feedback information that's still specific enough to be useful, without pointing to specific individuals

- sensitive feedback should be worded so as to not be offensive or accusatory

- no names should ever be linked to specific feedback items

- nothing a member says in an interview will be relayed back verbatim to the leader or any other member

Example:

Inappropriate Feedback	**_Feedback That Protects Confidentiality_**
Joe and Sally feel Fred is dictatorial.	20% of members expressed a desire for a more participative approach from the leader.

If a team member provides sensitive information, then insists that it can't be shared with the group, you need to work with that person to craft a statement that they feel can be shared. Members need to understand that an intervention is impossible unless people are willing to put their key points on the table.

Getting clear right at the start about confidentiality is important since effective interventions are only possible in an atmosphere of high trust. If the members of a team suspect that the person who's intervening is spreading stories, taking sides or acting as an agent of management, the intervention will not only be ineffective, but will likely worsen the situation.

Identifying the Client

The other key concept that must be clarified right at the start of any intervention, is that the person making the intervention is working for the *whole* team.

When a leader asks an outsider for assistance, he or she often assumes that the person making the intervention will see the leader as the client. He or she may even attempt to influence that person to see the situation from their perspective.

It's important, therefore, that the both the leader and the team members be told right at the start, that the person making the intervention is acting for the whole team.

The client for any intervention isn't the leader, but the whole team!

Clarifying the Role of the Person Intervening

Anyone making an intervention is expected to:

- be neutral
- work for the whole team

- provide a safe environment to give and receive feedback

- help the team assess its situation
- offer tools and techniques with which problems can be solved
- not be responsible for making improvements but work collaboratively with members to help them make improvements

- respect the view of all members
- keep control and make immediate interventions as needed
- guard the confidentiality of everyone who shares information
- act as a facilitator for group discussions

Anyone making interventions should also communicate that the secondary aim of every intervention is to provide a learning experience for the team's members so they can make their own interventions in the future.

Beware of Poor Interventions

Although the purpose of all interventions is to make a team's situation better, there are lots of examples of interventions that have made teams worse. That's because dealing with sensitive interpersonal issues always has the potential to lead to increased levels of conflict.

Beware of the following pitfalls. Doing any of these things will ensure that your next intervention is a disaster:

- Don't bother to do your research ahead of time, just guess at what the problem is.
- Pressure members to discuss sensitive issues out in the open even when they aren't ready to do so.
- Encourage the team to take on challenging tasks before the needed skills are in place.
- Don't bother creating the right atmosphere before asking people to share personal feedback.
- Let people attack each other in front of the group.
- Allow one person to be humiliated in front of the group.
- Keep going even when it's obvious the intervention isn't working as planned.

Because intervening is often quite sensitive, it has to be approached with adequate research and preparation. In the next chapter we provide you with a road map of the steps to take in properly planning and implementing any planned intervention.

Bibliography

Argyris, C. *Knowledge for Action.* San Francisco: Jossey-Bass, 1993.

—. *Overcoming Organizational Defences,* Boston: Allyn and Bacon, 1990.

Auvine, B., Densmore B., Extrom M., Poole S., and Shanklin M. *A Manual for Group Facilitators.* Madison, WI: Center for Conflict Resolution, 1978.

Avery, M., Auvine, B., Streibel B., and Weiss L. *Building United Judgement: A Handbook for Consensus Decision Making,* Madison WI: Center for Conflict Resolution, 1981.

Block, P. *Flawless Consulting.* San Diego: University Associates, 1981.

Bennis, W., and Shepard, H. "A Theory of Group Development." *Human Relations,* 1956.

Bradford, L. *Making Meetings Work.* San Diego: University Associates, 1976.

Dyer, W. *Team Building Issues and Alternatives.* Reading, MA: Addison-Wesley, 1977.

— . *Team Building,* 2nd Ed. Reading, MA: Addison-Wesley, 1987.

Filley, A.C. *Interpersonal Conflict Resolution.* Glenview, IL: Scott Foresman, 1975.

Fisher, R., and Ury, W. *Getting to Yes.* New York: Viking Press, 1991.

Hargrove, R. *Masterful Coaching.* San Diego: Pfeiffer & Company, 1995.

Katzenbach, J. and Smith, D. *The Wisdom of Teams.* New York: Harper Collins, 1993.

Kaufman, R. *Identifying and Solving Problems.* San Diego: University Associates, 1976.

Luft, J. *Group Processes: An Introduction to Group Dynamics.* Palo Alto, CA: National Press, 1963.

Reddy, B. *Intervention Skills: Process Consultation for Small Groups and Teams.* San Diego: Pfeiffer & Company, 1994.

Schein, E. and Bennis, W. *Personal and Group Change Through Group Methods.* New York: Wiley, 1965.

—. *Process Consultation: Its Role in Organization Development.* Reading, MA: Addison-Wesley, 1988.

Schwarz, R. *The Skilled Facilitator.* San Francisco: Jossey-Bass, 1994.

Short, J. and others. *The Social Psychology of Communication.* London: Wiley, 1976.

Stewart, J. *Bridges Not Walls.* Reading MA: Addison-Wesley, 1973.

Tuckman, B.W. , and Jensen, M.A.C. "Stages of Small Group Development Revisited." Group and Organizational Studies, 1977.

Walton, R., *Interpersonal Peacemaking: Confrontations and Third Party Consultation.* Reading MA: Addison-Wesley, 1969.

—. *Managing Conflict: Interpersonal Dialogue and Third Party Roles.* 2nd ed. Reading, MA: Addison-Wesley, 1987.

Intervention Steps

All interventions designed to help teams in trouble need to follow a series of steps. These steps ensure that the intervention is properly planned and implemented.

Steps in the Intervention Process

Step 1. Assessment
↓
Step 2. Planning
↓
Step 3. Contracting
↓
Step 4. Intervention
↓
Step 5. Follow-up

Using these steps is essential whether an intervention is made by the team leader, a member, or someone outside the team.

These steps guard against leaping to conclusions and implementing an intervention that doesn't address the real problems of the team.

What Happens in Each Step:

Step 1. Assessment: the person who'll be making the intervention, gathers, and assesses data about the team's situation.

Step 2. Planning: based on the data, the actual intervention activities are planned.

Step 3. Contracting: the person who'll be making the intervention shares the rough outline of the proposed intervention activities with the members of the team to get their suggestions and buy-in.

Step 4. Implementation: the proposed activities are conducted.

Step 5. Follow-up: the person who made the intervention follows up with the team after a specified time period to check on outcomes.

Step 1. Assessment

Thoroughly assessing the team's situation is a critical first step in making an effective intervention. Resist the urge to plunge in after a cursory glance at the team's situation. Neglecting to do an assessment sets the stage for making the wrong intervention.

Purpose of this Step

To gather data about the team's situation so that the appropriate set of intervention activities can be chosen.

Activities

One or more of the following activities <u>could</u> occur:

- conducting a focus group of some or all members
- interviewing individual team members
- observing the team in action
- conducting a survey
- interviewing or surveying key customers, members of other teams, or management representatives
- reading background materials

Challenges

- asking the right questions
- using the right assessment activity or tool
- listening actively
- understanding the problem from the perspective of the members
- building rapport and trust

Pitfalls

- not staying neutral
- jumping to conclusions
- accepting member assessments during the interviews to be true, without having all the data in front of you
- team members not disclosing all of the facts

Assessment Techniques

If you've been asked to make an intervention, either for your own or another team, your first step is to gather data about the team's problems so that you can design the right combination of intervention activities.

There are four main methods available to gather this information.

1. *Personal Interviews* - This involves having structured conversations with people, one at a time, to get individuals to open up and share their candid views of the situation. Most of these sessions are conducted in person, although they can be done over the phone. Most assessment interviews take from 20 to 40 minutes.

Depending on the situation, you might interview members of the team, the team leader, members of other teams, customers of the team, or senior managers.

The advantage of personal interviews is that people are more likely to open up and share sensitive information. The greatest disadvantage is the time consumed talking to members one at a time. In spite of the time issue, personal interviews are suggested whenever the intervention is likely to revolve around sensitive interpersonal relations.

The key to effective interviewing is remaining totally neutral, listening actively and asking good probing questions. It's bad practice to ask tricky or manipulative questions, or to appear to be agreeing with the assessment presented by each of the individuals. The best strategy is to be understanding but objective, while asking questions that focus on 'probing' the situation. Examples of good probing interview questions are offered on page 91.

2. *Focus Groups* - These are structured conversations held to gather information from a small group. Focus groups usually consist of four to ten people.

Focus group questions should be carefully structured so that the team's members are encouraged to openly discuss the issues facing the team. Responses should be recorded on a flipchart for all to see.

The advantage of focus groups is that the person making the intervention can observe the group's dynamics in action and determine the extent to which members agree on key issues. The disadvantage of focus groups is that people may not reveal sensitive information in front of a group. This means focus groups should be used when the team's problem isn't overly sensitive. The questions on page 91 will also be useful in planning a focus group session.

3. Surveys - This is a fundamental tool in making interventions. Using surveys involves interviewing a sample of team members and stakeholders in order to determine the types of questions that need to be asked, designing the survey, having members (anonymously) complete and return the survey, and tabulating the results.

There are a number of sample surveys provided in this manual. While some of these can be used straight from the book, most situations deserve their own custom designed survey.

Unlike interviews and focus groups, which use open-ended questions, surveys are based on closed-ended questions that either require a 'yes' or 'no,' or a rating scale response. This allows the results to be tabulated to provide data for the intervention.

When using a survey there are two possible ways to go about interpreting the data. The first way is to tabulate and interpret the data to find out which activities need to be implemented. An example of the appropriate use of this approach is assessing the results of a training needs survey in order to design a series of workshops.

The second approach is to gather individual responses onto a blank survey sheet and return it to the members for their assessment. This approach is very effective when there's a problem that team members need to solve. By getting members to make their own assessment, they're more likely to accept the survey results, than if you do it for them.

4. Observation - Observing a team in action is a powerful way of understanding the dimensions affecting both interpersonal and group dynamics. This assessment method involves getting the team's permission to observe them during one of their regular meetings, then sitting silently in the background to make notes. This approach can be used even by someone who is a regular member of a team. It's usually impossible to become aware of group dynamics without watching from the side-lines!

The advantage of observing a team in action is that it allows us to see how people treat each other, the level of participation, how the team makes decisions, handles power and so forth. The disadvantage of relying only on information gathered from observations is that members may become self-conscious and be on their best behavior, while the real problems lay hidden.

Observing team process is a good idea for any intervention that concerns group dynamics, conflict, meeting effectiveness, and the role of the leader.

Sample Assessment Questions

The following are generic questions that are commonly asked in interviews, with focus groups or on surveys. Please remember that these questions are completely out of context and should not be used as they're presented here. There are also far too many questions provided here. Most 30 minute interviews revolve around four or five key questions that are consistently asked of all respondents.

- *Tell me the story of this team's current situation in your own words?*

- *What adjectives would you use to describe the team climate?*

- *How would others describe this problem? Take the perspective of the customer, other teams, senior managers, etc.*

- *On a scale of one to five, how serious would you say the current situation is?*

1	2	3	4	5
Serious		Somewhat serious		Very serious

- *How is the situation currently being managed? What's been tried and with what results?*

- *What are the barriers to making needed improvements?*

- *Who wants change to take place? Who doesn't?*

- *How do you personally contribute to the team's problems?*

- *What skills, resources, intervention activities or other changes do you think will improve the team's effectiveness?*

- *How willing and motivated are others on the team to resolve this situation?*

- *What fears or concerns do you have about the intervention? What could go wrong?*

- *What rules, conditions or other assurances do you need to feel really comfortable participating freely and honestly?*

- *Are there any proposals for change that would be taboo or unacceptable?*

- *If the current situation were to be totally resolved, what would the team look like?*

- *What adjectives would you use to describe this team if it were ideal?*

- *What would be the best contribution I could make to this process? What do you expect from me? What's the biggest mistake I could make?*

Known and Hidden Factors Worksheet

A good place to start when developing interview, focus group or survey questions is to write down what you've been told so far – *what's known*, and what you've not been told – *what's hidden.*

What are all of the obvious, stated facts of this case?	What are all the things that are unknown or hidden?
Known	**Hidden**

When Interviewing People Before an Intervention

- Check out your assumptions concerning your client and your client organization before your interviews. During the early stages, ask yourself: *What preconceptions do I have that are unfounded and stem from personal biases and prejudices?*

- Aim for communication that is open, direct, precise, and as simple as possible.

- Practice empathetic or active listening throughout the process. Don't be afraid to ask for clarification of the issue at any stage.

- Use body language that portrays openness and directness in a friendly manner. Maintain eye contact and use an open body posture.

- Ensure that there are no interruptions during any interviews.

- Be assertive. Express yourself without putting others down, without patronizing, and without violating the other's sense of self worth.

- In making recommendations, be careful when use of the expressions, *"you should..."* and *"you ought to..."* since they can be taken offensively and create resistance.

- Communicate from a position of active orientation to the issue. Maintain control throughout by initiating, paraphrasing, clarifying, directing, summarizing, etc.

- Become aware of the communication space between you and your client. Notice its effects and change it if necessary (i.e., physical distance, obstructions such as a desk and differences in seat elevation are some aspects of communication space).

- Deal openly and honestly in the face of resistance, such as avoidance on the part of the client to accept responsibility for the problem, taking the subject off-track, etc.

- Put a constant effort into making the client feel comfortable and into projecting (through words and body language) your positive feelings towards the client and your desire for a positive outcome.

- Notice your own psychological blocks to using clear and direct communication and deal with them apart from the interview (i.e., lack of confidence, poor self esteem, fear of rejection, apprehension).

- Trust your intuition and learn to rely on it to identify the problem and to assess the ongoing process.

- Don't be afraid to reveal yourself (i.e., *"I feel confused right now. Would you clarify what you've just said?"* or *"I would like that suggestion."* or *"I don't feel that we've progressed very far. Do you feel the same?"*).

Conducting an Interview

Here's a quick checklist to help you remember the key points of effective interviewing:

__ Be warm and friendly. Take some time for friendly chatter to establish rapport.

__ Make eye contact. Really listen. Show empathy.

__ Clearly state and confirm the purpose of the meeting and set adequate time aside to complete it.

__ State your understanding of the problem based on what you've been told so far.

__ Ask questions, paying careful attention to body language and the client's responsiveness.

__ Paraphrase and clarify main points made by client.

__ Delve more deeply into key points.

__ Make observations that help the client to delve more deeply.

__ Clarify what the client wants and needs from the consultation.

__ Clarify what you bring to the process (i.e., expertise/experience).

__ Make sure the client does most of the talking.

__ Don't judge, evaluate, or reach too quick a conclusion.

__ Help the client clarify feelings. Validate these feelings.

__ Check to see if the client is satisfied with the progress of the interview.

__ Discuss and negotiate any other research (i.e., surveys, staff interviews, reading, focus groups) you need in order to progress.

__ Sum up what the client has told you so far to assure clarity.

__ Confirm next steps.

Interview Observation Worksheet

Use the following to debrief your own interview effectiveness.

Effective Behaviors	**Did I do this (Y or N)?**
Did the interviewer ...	*Describe the occasions ...*
... appear very clear about the meeting's purpose?	
...seem to really care about the needs and concerns of the team members?	
...focus on member's needs rather than on his/her own needs or 'expert' opinions?	
...ask the kind of questions that helped the members see things fully and realistically?	
...establish his or her credentials when required?	
...work together collaboratively with the people being interviewed?	
...periodically check to see if the member's needs were being met?	
...create a warm and friendly atmosphere?	
...help the team members clarify what they want to achieve?	
...encourage honest disclosure of concerns and problems?	
...deal with difficult interpersonal situations directly and forthrightly?	
...really listen to what was said as well as paraphrase key ideas?	
...structure the discussion so that the members do most of the talking?	
...seem open to team member input?	
...clarify his/her assumptions and perceptions?	
...support, rather than judge the members?	
...help to clarify feelings when they arose?	
...refrain from jumping to conclusions and/or 'advising'?	

Step 2. Planning

Interventions are always complex activities that need to be carefully designed. Remember that professional facilitators spend one hour preparing, for every hour spent in front of a group. Once you've prepared your preliminary design, it needs to be shared with the team to gain their buy-in. This is usually a short meeting (15-30 minutes) in which you present highlights of the data collected and the proposal for the planned intervention. This is helpful because team members will give you valuable feedback about how well your design fits their situation.

Purpose of this Step

- to interpret the data collected in Step #1.

- to decide on the type(s) of intervention activities needed.

Activities

- assessing data collected in Step #1

- selecting the appropriate intervention activities

- designing the objectives and the agenda of the proposed intervention session

Challenges

- making an accurate assessment of the data
- correctly sequencing the activities

Pitfalls

- insufficient preparation before the session

- underestimating that people might be reluctant or sensitive

- pushing ahead with activities that members say they can't handle

- not having a fallback strategy or alternative activities ready in case the intervention plan is challenged

Intervention Planning Worksheet #1

When all of the data has been collected, you need to assess it and prepare a preliminary outline of the proposed intervention. Refer to the sample interventions starting on page 143 for suggestions on how to design an intervention.

What is the data saying? What are the major issues and needs?

What one or two-sentence statement would clearly describe the current situation?

What, if any, are the sensitive aspects of this intervention?

What blocks or barriers should you anticipate? What else could go wrong?

Describe the type(s) of intervention that you will propose (i.e., re-forming the team, training, problem solving, feedback, coaching, mediation)?

Briefly outline the specific intervention activities that you think will be effective?

What's the desired outcome of the intervention? Write an *outcome statement* that describes how a successful intervention will impact the team.

Intervention Planning Worksheet #2

Briefly outline below the specific intervention activities that you intend to do, in the sequence you think will be most appropriate.

Activity	Time Required
1.	
2.	
3.	
4.	
5.	
6.	
7.	

How long will the intervention take? Will it all be achieved in one session?

Step 3. Contracting

Even though an intervention may not be a voluntary activity, it's important to gain member buy-in. A week or so before the actual intervention takes place, it's important to preview the planned activities with the team to get their reactions, suggestions, and support. If there's going to be resistance to the intervention, it's a good idea to find out in advance. This allows time to redesign activities or at least lets you know to what extent you'll need to work through resistance.

Purpose of this Step
- present the proposed intervention to get team member comments and suggestions
- set mutual expectations and get buy-in
- establish any boundaries for the intervention
- clarify the roles of the parties
- discuss any challenging aspects and develop contingencies

Activities
- a face-to-face meeting between the members and the person who'll be conducting the intervention
- a brief sharing of data collected
- a presentation of the proposed activities
- team members react, comment, offer suggestions
- adjustments are made to the intervention
- creation of a mutual *outcome statement*
- agreement about next steps, time, and place

Challenges
- reaching the right conclusions
- dealing with the difference between what the members want and actually need
- members who reject the proposed intervention out of fear or other personal reasons
- unrealistic expectations on the part of the members or the leader
- presenting sensitive information in a totally neutral manner

Pitfalls
- not uncovering the 'truth' of the situation
- going along with an intervention idea that members want but don't need
- proposing an activity that members can't handle
- not listening to their ideas and input
- going ahead with unrealistic expectations

Proposing a Course of Action

One of the most valuable contributions of anyone making an intervention is helping the team see the true nature of their situation. Team members are often too close to their problem to be objective. It often takes the feeding back of data, before members come to grips with reality.

Since we all tend to see things differently and since sensitive information is difficult to share, it's important that you choose your words very carefully. You should also be prepared to deal with rejection of your assessment and resistance to your proposals.

The Preview Meeting

A week or so before making the intervention, it's important to go to a team meeting and take some time to share your findings to get member reaction to the proposed intervention. Here's how to structure that meeting:

1. Share the original problem statement. Summarize what you were originally told was the team's problem. Keep this very simple.

Example: The team has difficulties meeting deadlines and everyone is constantly scrambling to get their work done. Several members have had conflicts over workloads and there's now some tension at the weekly team meetings.

2. Give a data summary. Share a very brief summary of the data collected. Don't provide more than you need to justify your choice of intervention activities at this meeting.

Example: The team never held a team launch meeting to establish clear objectives, priorities and joint work plans. There are no clear work priorities in place. Members all have different amounts of work to do, with no strategy to link those with too much work to those who have less. Conflicts about the workload issue have never been resolved.

3. Explain the type(s) of intervention needed. Describe which of the six types of activities you think the team needs. Again provide just the broad outline of the proposed activities.

Example: I propose that the team revisit *Team Launch* (Type #1). This will include establishing clear objectives and results measures, setting priorities, doing joint work planning, clarifying roles and responsibilities.

The team should then do some *problem solving* (Type #3). This will consist of working together to find solutions to the problem of unscheduled 'firefighting' type assignments that crop up daily.

The members also need to *give and receive feedback* (Type #4). This would be a structured written exercise that lets members give each other feedback about how they could work together more effectively.

4. Ask for feedback. Ask members for their reaction to the proposed activities and take into account any suggestions they offer. Answer any questions and ask if people have any concerns or reservations. One way to do this is to ask members to identify what could go wrong or be difficult. Record these concerns on the right half of a flipchart. On the left side, ask members to offer suggestions to alleviate each item in the concern column. Stop when you have at least one suggestion for each concern. These will form a base set of norms for the intervention session.

5. Facilitate the formation of an outcome statement. Ask each person to write down a statement that describes the best possible outcome of the intervention. Go around the room and collect key points. Merge these together to create a statement that represents what the team wants to get out of the session.

6. Clarify next steps. dentify the time, date, duration, and place of the session. Clarify your role. Thank the members for their cooperation and express optimism that their intervention will be beneficial.

Dealing with Resistance

There are a whole range of possible reasons why a team member might resist or even reject your intervention proposals when you present them.

- your data collection may be incomplete
- your assessment may be wrong
- they may be unwilling to face a serious problem or confront specific members of the team
- they may feel threatened by the depth of the intervention proposed
- they may be unwilling to do what it takes to make change once they have identified how much work it'll take to fix things
- problem individuals may simply want to block the team from solving its issues, especially if the intervention is likely to focus on them

If it turns out that you didn't collect enough information or that you made an incorrect assessment, the input you receive at the contracting session might stop you from planning an inappropriate intervention.

If on the other hand, team members resist because they feel that the proposed activities are too risky or sensitive, you need to surface their concerns at this time. The best way of dealing with reluctance is to ask members to identify the conditions under which they would be willing to go ahead with what you propose. They might say they'll participate as long as no one is personally attacked or as long as all feedback is constructive. You should record these conditions and build your intervention around them. These conditions become part of the norms for the session (for more on *Safety Norms* see page 113).

If you suspect members are resisting to avoid doing the right thing, you need to take a slightly different approach. Listen actively to their rejection of your proposal and paraphrase what you hear, even if you totally disagree. Then stand firm and repeat what you think they need to do. Remember that there's often a gap between what the team wants and what it needs. One strategy is to leave your proposal with the team and allow them some time to come to grips with what you're suggesting. You may even need to negotiate by giving in on some of their wants, in order to get them to address their real needs. Remember, it's your job to help the team do what's really needed.

The bottom-line is you shouldn't shy away from doing what's needed just to keep team members comfortable. In fact it's quite legitimate to decline the assignment of making an intervention if the team refuses to do what's really needed, or if the activities they're proposing have a likelihood of being counter-productive.

Dealing with Resistance at at Feedback Session

Anyone who has ever given feedback knows how very difficult a task it is. In fact giving feedback is often more stressful on the person giving it than on the person at the receiving end.

To foster an environment where feedback is both easy to give and to receive, consider adopting the following rules when you are on the receiving end of feedback.

Listen actively:	Paraphrase if you can. Ask probing questions to make sure you understand what is being said to you.
Don't get emotional:	Breathe deeply. Sit back. Adopt relaxed body language. Look the speaker in the eye. Lower your voice. Speak slowly.
Don't get defensive:	This isn't aimed at you personally. Understand the other person's perspective before you present your side of the story.
Accept the input:	Do this even if you don't agree with all of it. It shows respect of the other person's perspective.
Work hard on improvements:	Spend your energy on finding improvements rather than disputing the observations. Do not put all of the burden for finding solutions on the other person, offer some ideas.

When the intervention being proposed is based on a sound diagnosis and the team is truly facing an issue they *must* address, then the intervenor needs to become assertive in pressing for the planned activity.

This often means dealing with resistance. When the client 'pushes back' from an activity in spite of the fact that it's appropriate, the consultant should:

1. Identify what form the resistance is taking. What specifically are they reacting to? What is the fear?

2. In a neutral, non-judgmental way, state what you see...

   "I notice that you've all become quiet and are looking at each other with concern."
   ...or
   "From the last two comments I am getting the message that you don't want to give each other feedback about personal performance on the team."

This is called *naming the resistance.*

3. Be quiet after your assessment. Use the silence. Let the client respond.

4. Paraphrase what they say. Empathize with their views.

5. Clearly and affirmatively state your position. Explain clearly why you are recommending this course of action or have made this assessment.

6. Answer all questions. Help the members understand the need for the intervention activity.

If these series of steps don't get them over their barriers, move them forward by facilitating the discussion on the next page.

Naming the Resistance

When the Resistance Takes this Form	Name it by Making this Statement
Client's avoiding responsibility for the problem or the solution	*"You don't see yourself as a part of the problem."*
Flooding you with detail	*"You are giving me more detail than I need. How would you describe it in a short statement?"*
One-word answers	*"You are giving me very short answers. Could you say more?"*
Changing the subject	*"The subject keeps shifting. Could we stay focused on one area at a time?"*
Compliance	*"You seem willing to do anything I suggest. I can't tell what your feelings are"*
Silence	*"You are very quiet. I don't know how to read your silence."*
Press for solutions	*"I think that it's too early for solutions. I'm still trying to find out..."*
Attack	*"You are really questioning a lot of what I do. You seem angry about something."*

Facilitating Teams Through Resistance

When a whole team balks at a needed intervention, they may have a legitimate concern. You will then need to facilitate a discussion using the following process:

1. Divide the members into subgroups if they seem afraid to speak in a large group. Ask them to appoint recorders to report back at the end of their discussion.

2. Give them about five minutes per question as described below.

3. Then leave the room so they can work alone.

These two questions represent the basic facilitation technique for dealing with resistance:

Question #1. What and why are you resisting?
(This lets them surface their worries and vent their concerns in the safety of a small group.)

Question #2. What will make you willing to move forward with this activity?
(This places the ball in their court. They spell out the conditions under which they would be willing to participate.)

When the team reports back with their answers to the two questions, you can then respond to their concerns. The team is now basically negotiating the conditions of their participation. Not surprisingly, the things they need are most often measures that will guarantee their 'safety' throughout the activity.

If this fails and the team continues to resist the activities they need, the person attempting to make the intervention may need to quit.

Contracting Checklist

Here's a summary of the steps involved in *contracting*.

___ Make a personal statement of your feelings about being in this meeting with the client to increase the personal comfort level between yourself and the client. (i.e., "This is an area in which I have a special interest. I'm pleased to be involved.")

___ Restate the original request received from the team members to confirm mutual understanding of the situation.

___ Ask if you can present the data you gathered. Proceed to share your findings. Stay very objective, especially about sensitive areas.

___ Clarify any questions from the team members. Don't challenge or sound superior or judgmental.

___ State your diagnosis of the situation and offer your proposal for intervention.

___ Reassure the members that you can help find a solution or make a referral if you don't think you can help.

___ Ask directly how they see the situation in light of the data.

___ Find out if they have specific notions as to how you should proceed and what constraints there are on the project (i.e., time lines, access to people in the organization, access to information, confidentiality, budget).

___ Ask members directly what they want from you (i.e., recommendations, a study, training, expert help, advice, etc.).

___ Find out who else is/should be involved?

___ State what you have to offer (i.e., a clear picture of the issue, experience with similar problems, etc.).

___ After exchanging 'wants,' restate the agreement you've reached.

___ Find out how committed the team is to the intervention.

___ Find out if the team feels they have sufficient control over how the intervention is going to proceed.

___ Give genuine and specific support to the team for their willingness to proceed with the intervention.

___ Reach agreement on next steps.

Characteristics of a Strong Contract

At the end of a successful contracting discussion:

- everyone is satisfied that the intervention is based on sound data
- all parties feel a high level of commitment to the activities described
- the details (i.e., time, place, roles, preparation) are clear
- anxieties and possible risks have been openly discussed
- the members and the person making the intervention have good feelings about each other.

A Contract is Weak When:

- the intervention design isn't supported by the data collected
- the team's ability to invest the time required and commitment to follow-through are in question
- the intervention is a low priority because of time and work pressures
- the team or the leader is trying to abdicate major responsibility to the person making the intervention
- it feels like members aren't openly discussing their concerns and reservations
- people don't trust the competence or personality of the person intervening.

Putting it in Writing

Once there is verbal agreement about the nature of the intervention, it's important to summarize key points in a brief memo. This lessens the possibility of misunderstandings later on. The memo doesn't have to be more than a page or two and should include:

- background to the request
- data assessment
- agreed to approach and activities
- parameters and constraints
- time frame and schedule
- expected result
- role clarification
- next step
- closing comments

On the following page is a sample contracting memorandum.

Sample Contracting Memo

To: All Members of the Order Fulfillment Team

Further to our meeting, the following summarizes our discussions about the upcoming intervention.

Background to this Intervention - the Order Fulfillment Team was formed within the Finance Department two years ago to expedite the processing of orders generated by the company's top ten customers. The team had been working effectively for most of that time, but lately the team has become quite ineffective at getting its work done on time. As a result of these pressures, there are interpersonal tensions among members for the first time. There's also growing concern that meetings have become more frustrating, with less output.

Data Assessment - member interviews and a survey have revealed the following: Concerning team workloads: members have become unclear about their role and responsibilities on the team, workloads are described by the majority of members as inequitable and there is growing slippage on meeting critical deadlines. Concerning meetings: people come and go throughout most meetings, agendas are poorly planned and important decisions often end in stalemates or strife.

Proposed Approach - a combined approach:
- to re-form the team, by clarifying roles, responsibilities and redoing the team's work plans
- to solve the issue of uneven workloads by identifying and removing the main barriers
- to hold a training session on meeting management and decision-making

Parameters and Constraints - from our discussions I understand that:
- the intervention should take place immediately
- the team has a total of only two hours during their next two team meetings to deal with these issues

Time Frame and Schedule - the two, 2-hour sessions will take place from 8:30 - 10:30 a.m. during the team's next two regularly scheduled meetings: September 12 and 19, in Conference Room A.

Expected Results - at the end of these two sessions, the team expects:
- clarity about member roles and responsibilities
- a more equitable distribution of workloads among members
- more effective use of consensus and voting to make decisions
- meetings that end on time with all agenda items addressed

My role: to plan all intervention activities, to prepare the meeting agenda, to identify all resource materials, and to facilitate the two, 2-hour sessions.

Your role: to ensure all members receive information about the session, to photocopy the handouts and training materials, to rent the selected training video and to make all room arrangements.

Next steps: I will forward the agenda, training materials and worksheets to you for photocopying by the Thursday before each session.

I have enjoyed meeting the members of this team and look forward to assisting you to make this team even more effective than it has been in the past.

Sincerely,

_____

Your name

Step 4. Implementation

Conducting an intervention is never simple or easy. Always expect that the session might be tense and difficult to facilitate. The person making an intervention always needs to be alert to changes in the group and ready to make immediate interventions as needed.

Purpose of this Step:
- to conduct the agreed to intervention activities so as to greatly improve the condition of the team

Activities:
- creating the proper atmosphere for the intervention
- sharing data collected in the assessment stage
- facilitating the intervention activities
- evaluating member satisfaction at the end of the activity
- deciding on next steps and follow-up activities

Challenges:
- setting the right tone for the intervention
- keeping people 'safe' throughout
- team members suddenly withdrawing their buy-in
- team members withholding their true feelings
- deteriorating team dynamics
- keeping one finger on the pulse of the group to monitor member feelings
- staying really flexible and willing to alter the intervention as it unfolds, to meeting changing needs and circumstances
- the suggestions and commitments made by the members may fall short of what is needed to really resolve the situation

Pitfalls:
- not establishing clear and realistic expectations
- not getting clear buy-in from all members
- plunging ahead with the agenda even when it seems obvious the intervention isn't working as designed
- not having an alternative course of action on hand
- not putting in the effort needed
- not staying neutral
- lapsing into a directive mode and telling the members what to do

Starting the Intervention

By the time you actually conduct the intervention, if you've done your homework you'll have:

- met most or all of the team members
- identified the deeper issues behind the original request
- created a set of interactive activities that address the issues
- gained input and commitment from the members to participate honestly and energetically
- have a number of alternative activities on hand in case any part of the agenda doesn't work out as planned.

Getting Started

The following sequence of activities will help you get started:

- begin by thanking the members for the opportunity of assisting them
- state the problem you were originally asked to help with
- review the data collection from prepared flipchart sheets; post these notes on a wall
- review the agenda for the session
- facilitate a discussion about the norms or rules that ought to be in place for this special session; bring back any notes from the preview meeting
- if members will be making sensitive comments to each other, provide some training on the kind of body language and wording that's most appropriate
- begin the intervention by providing clear instructions for all activities and discussions

Remember:

An intervention is a problem situation. Something has gone wrong, so this session can't be expected to be a fun and breezy meeting. Members need to understand and accept that this could be tough, and that that's okay. Create some safety features like empowering any member to call a time-out or ask for a break if things get overly emotional, but don't buckle at the first sign of tension.

As the person making the intervention you must maintain your calm and composure. At the same time it's a good strategy to openly acknowledge any tensions you might be feeling. This reassures people that it's acceptable to feel stressed. Remember that your behavior will serve as a model for the whole team.

Sharing Data with Team Members

Feeding back information, especially when there are sensitive issues on the table, requires careful and clear communication.

When reporting data, the consultant has two distinct choices, **A** or **B**:

A	B
Interpret the data and present a summary of conclusions	***Share the raw data and have the participants interpret its meaning***
<u>**Interpreted Feedback**</u>	<u>**Survey Feedback**</u>
You sort out the things people said were working well and report on them first.	You tabulate, interview, and survey responses onto a single sheet.
You then name the team's issues based on the data.	This raw data is then given to the team.
Example: Your comments at the interviews indicate that there is widespread dissatisfaction with meetings, particularly the lack of structure and tendency to get side-tracked.	***Example:*** here are the ratings from the survey: • *What do you think the results say is going well?* • *What are the problem items?* • *Why do you think these items received these low ratings?*

Both approaches then evolve into problem identification and systematic problem-solving exercises.

What do you think are the pro's and con's of each approach? When would you use either?

_____

_____

_____

_____

Using Safety Norms

While the team you're with may already have an excellent set of team rules or *norms*, most teams need new norms for a meeting as sensitive as an intervention.

That's because people will likely be required to give and receive feedback about sensitive matters. The norms required for an intervention help people feel 'safe' throughout the discussion, while still allowing them to discuss issues freely.

You can generate *safety norms* by asking one or more of the following questions:

> *"What assurances do you need to be able to freely express your feelings and views about the current situation?"*

> *"What behaviors do we need to commit to for today's session?"*

> *"What rules will help us ensure that our comments won't ever get personal or negative?"*

> *"What do we agree to do if we get into conflict or things suddenly get heated?"*

Here's a sample set of some safety norms:

- all discussions are strictly confidential — nothing leaves this room
- both people and issues will be handled with respect
- everyone will be sincere and honest
- no one will personally attack another team member
- anyone giving feedback about another person must look them in the eye while speaking
- all feedback has to be objective, factual and have a constructive element
- anyone who feels overly stressed can ask for a 'time out'
- everyone will be an active listener and not interrupt others
- we will immediately stop talking if several people start talking at once
- everyone has to act out of positive intent to improve the team

The above sample norms are intended only as an illustration. Remember that the only norms that really work for a team are the ones they create for themselves.

Interpersonal Techniques for Team Members

Sadly, members of teams in trouble often lack the basic skills of effective teamwork. These members may not know how to address each other in an appropriate and respectful manner or how to give and receive feedback graciously. The need for open dialogue is especially critical during an intervention. If the participants are rude or make snide comments during the session, the problems of the team could worsen.

Before launching into any intervention activity, it's always wise to offer teams the following guidelines. Please note that these should not be presented as optional – don't be shy about telling member how they must behave.

Here are some useful tips to share with the group:

• Anyone being spoken to by another member must give that member their full and courteous attention. Keep constant eye contact and resist negative body language. No interruptions allowed.

• Anyone responding to a point of disagreement must first restate the key points made by the other person before beginning to present their point of view. Example:

> *"You're saying that the meeting room was a mess three days in a row after I had last used it. Can I tell you my version of that situation?"*

• Always stick to the facts of any situation and never attribute motives or make accusations based on assumptions about another person. Example:

> *"You were late getting me the data I asked you for in April and May"...is better than "You never bother to meet my deadlines."*

• Members can and should report on the impact problems have had on them, but need to do this without rancor. Example:

> *"When your numbers were late, I had to work overtime the next three nights to meet my deadline." ...is better than "You don't seem to care that you create a lot of extra work for me."*

During the Intervention

Because interventions can get off track easily, it's important to do periodic checks throughout the session. **To check the process, periodically ask members:**

> *"Is this working?"*
>
> *"Are we getting anywhere?"*
>
> *"Is this technique effective?"*

If there are problems with the process, you'll get some feedback and be able to make changes on the spot. It's a really terrible idea to forge ahead with any activity that isn't working. **To check the pace, ask members:**

> *"Is this going too slow?"*
>
> *"Is this going too fast?"*

If they indicate either of the above, immediately discuss what they think can be done and then adopt any ideas that sound good. If you have an idea about how to improve the pace, suggest it after the members have had their chance to comment first. Make sure they approve of your suggestions before you implement them.

Check the members. 'Hold up a mirror' periodically and tell them what you see. Make these statements very non-judgmental by reporting just what you see:

> *"Three people are writing notes and haven't said anything for ten minutes."*
>
> *"Four of you are wearing concerned expressions right now."*

Be careful not to jump to conclusions. In the last example, if you say: *"Four of you look worried,"* they may correct you to say they're not worried, just concentrating. It's better to report more simply on what you see and ask them what it means. Once they have interpreted what the body language means, you can respond more accurately to improve their participation. Example:

> *"We're not concerned, just tired."*
> *(This may mean they need to take a break).*
>
> *"I'm not listening because I don't think we're dealing with the right issue."*
> *(This may mean refocusing the conversation of the team).*

Ending the Intervention

At the end of any intervention, it's good practice to:

- summarize the key points that have been made

- clarify the specific next steps and other commitments made by the team

- ensure that there are detailed action plans in place for all follow-up items

- end on a positive note by congratulating the team for the manner in which they've conducted themselves and the results achieved

- thank the team for the opportunity of participating

- ask the members to complete the intervention evaluation form and leave it behind

- offer to tabulate the post intervention evaluation meeting

- tell them that you'll be in contact with them in the weeks ahead to see how they're progressing, and

- offer your ongoing assistance should they require it.

Note: It's best if the facilitator doesn't take home the action plans or offer to write up the notes from the session. The ownership for the intervention outcomes should rest with the team. It's best if one of the team's members takes responsibility for finalizing and circulating the notes.

Seeking Personal Feedback

A powerful modeling technique is to ask the team members for personal feedback at the end of the session. This creates further credibility for you and sets a great example of the values and attitudes of interventions.

The following two questions can be answered verbally with the whole team, or you can leave the room and return after the team members have discussed them. In either case, you will get to hear what members have to say about your performance.

The two feedback questions:

What did I do very effectively in planning and running this session?
What could I have done differently or better?

Planning for Action

One firm rule for ending an intervention is that the team must leave with at least some action plans in their hands. These plans have to spell out what and how it'll be done, by when and by whom. Members have to assume the lion's share of responsibility for making sure these actions are carried out, monitored, and reported back to the team.

The follow-up actions to which we are committing include:

What	How	By Whom	By When

Intervention Evaluation Form

Please provide your anonymous evaluation concerning today's workshop.

1. What do you think we accomplished?

_____

_____

_____

2. What did you personally:

Like	Dislike

3. What feedback would you like to give to the facilitator?

_____

_____

_____

4. Overall, how would you rate today's activity:

1	2	3	4	5
It hurt us!	Poor	Satisfactory	Good	It really helped!

5. Additional Comments:

_____

_____

_____

Step 5. Follow-up

Teams are more likely to follow through on their plans if they know that there'll be an evaluation activity.

Purpose of this Step

- to check on the long term outcome of the intervention to assess whether or not the activities conducted were effective

- to keep open the lines of communication

- to explore further intervention needs of the team

- to provide a forum to offer further assistance

Activities

One or more of the following:

- informal calls to check on progress

- a face-to-face visit with team members

- a written survey of members

- a written summary

Challenges

- the tendency to talk about problems but fail to take corrective action

- getting the team members to monitor and report on their own progress

Pitfalls

- not bothering to monitor progress

- not reporting on the results

- lack of honesty in the final assessment

- not doing the needed follow-up intervention activities

Monitoring and Evaluating Results

Since the ownership of any intervention always rests with the team, the person making the intervention isn't always aware of the final outcome. It's quite appropriate, therefore, for you to call the original contact person and find out what's happened to the team.

It's also appropriate to ask whether or not the team needs further support and to recommend additional intervention activities. You cannot, however, dictate whether or not a further intervention takes place. That decision rests with the team.

Several weeks after an intervention, you may wish to ask the team to complete a follow-up evaluation form to help them assess how the activities impacted them in the long run. A sample post-intervention evaluation form is provided on the next page.

Intervention Summary Report

You can bring closure to any intervention by summarizing the evaluative comments in a brief memo. This can include such things as:

- actions implemented by the team

- impacts of the intervention on the members

- other signs the intervention worked

- negative impacts of the intervention

- remaining issues needing resolution

- recommended next steps

When the intervention is major and considerable follow-up is involved, it may be advisable to use a longer, more formal reporting format, a sample of which follows.

Sample Post-Intervention Team Member Evaluation

On June 3rd, your team met to resolve its issues of work distribution and role clarity. Some weeks have now passed and it's important that we stop to assess how successful those efforts have been.

Please complete the following questions anonymously and return it to Peter by Friday, April 8, at 4:00 p.m. Your frank and constructive comments are most appreciated.

1. What would you say has been improved as a result of the intervention?

_____

_____

_____

2. Has anything actually been made worse by the intervention?

_____

_____

_____

3. Is there anything that remains a problem in spite of the intervention?

_____

_____

_____

4. What further action do we need to take on this subject? Do we need another intervention? If so, what do you recommend?

_____

_____

_____

Additional Comments:

_____

_____

Intervention Progress Report

Date: _____ Name of Team: _____

Name of Initiative: _____

Current Stage in Implementation: _____

Progress To Date

Specific Activities Completed	Results Achieved

Activities Remaining

What still needs to be done?	By whom?	By when?

Comments: _____

_____

_____

Signed: _____

Intervention Skills Inventory

This is an exercise you can do to help you identify your strengths, plus the skills you need to develop.

Step I: Please look at each item and rate yourself by placing a check in one of the columns. If an item isn't applicable write N/A beside it.

Step II: When you've rated yourself on all items, please review your ratings. Place an asterisk in the column beside those which you need more skill in and are a priority in your work.

Step III: From amongst those you marked with an asterisk, select no more than six as priorities for your personal learning. Please write these six out on the last page of the questionnaire.

Intervention Skills Inventory

	I have the skills to do this	I need more skills in this area
Gathering Information		
1. Asking the right fact-finding questions	_____	_____
2. Clarifying what the member(s) means through paraphrasing, feedback data, etc.	_____	_____
3. Being open, objective, non-judgmental	_____	_____
Giving Information		
1. Clearly stating my intentions and objectives at the start	_____	_____
2. Disclosing my feelings if appropriate	_____	_____
3. Giving advice in an appropriate manner	_____	_____
4. Preparing written reports	_____	_____
5. Doing oral presentations	_____	_____
Establishing Relationships		
1. Listening for facts and feelings	_____	_____
2. Checking for understanding	_____	_____

3. Clarifying roles and relationships   _____   _____

4. Offering feedback   _____   _____

5. Asking for feedback   _____   _____

6. Dealing with my anger   _____   _____

7. Dealing with others' anger   _____   _____

8. Confronting people if need be   _____   _____

Transferring Skills

1. Helping member(s) to diagnose
    own skills   _____   _____

2. Helping member(s) learn how to
    identify and solve problems   _____   _____

3. Helping the team to use
    planning procedures and tools   _____   _____

4. Helping member(s) take risks   _____   _____

5. Helping the team identify resources   _____   _____

Entry Skills

1. Setting clear and appropriate objectives
    for my first meeting with the team   _____   _____

2. Establishing my credibility   _____   _____

3. Collecting information about current
    practices, assumptions, problems   _____   _____

4. Helping member(s) talk about their
    fears and reservations   _____   _____

5. Helping member(s) identify key issues   _____   _____

6. Identifying the appropriate consulting style   _____   _____

Contracting Skills

1. Identifying realistic outcomes with
    the team's input   _____   _____

2. Presenting my biases   _____   _____

3. Saying *no* and explaining why   _____   _____

4. Working through a mutual understanding   _____   _____
to an appropriate contract and action plan

5. Talking about my reservations and   _____   _____
concerns about the contract

6. Soliciting the member(s) reservations   _____   _____
and/or concerns about the contract

7. Identifying roles and responsibilities   _____   _____

8. Clarifying restraints and limitations   _____   _____

9. Scheduling action, reviewing, and   _____   _____
checking points

10. Giving feedback about the meeting so far   _____   _____

11. Asking for feedback about the   _____   _____
meeting so far

Problem-Solving

1. Identifying problems using several methods   _____   _____

2. Separating problem-identification from   _____   _____
problem-solving

3. Relating information to other organizational   _____   _____
issues (i.e., structure, power, authority,
constraints, etc.)

4. Identifying criteria to select the best   _____   _____
alternative solution

5. Identifying several solutions   _____   _____

6. Setting out the costs and risks of   _____   _____
each solution

7. Using appropriate data collecting techniques   _____   _____

8. Seeking data to confirm or discount   _____   _____
my hunches

Diagnosis and Analysis Skills

1. Using interviews, questionnaires, or other   _____   _____
   means to assess needs

2. Interpreting survey results   _____   _____

3. Paying attention to both facts and feelings   _____   _____

4. Differentiating between *"what I see"* and   _____   _____
   "what the team member sees"

Planning Skills

1. Presenting the analysis and alternative plans   _____   _____

2. Facilitating understanding of alternative plans   _____   _____

3. Helping the team distinguish between   _____   _____
   "what is necessary" and *"what is desirable"*

4. Encouraging the team member to   _____   _____
   express feelings about the plans

5. Relating activities to organizational goals   _____   _____

Planning for Action

1. Helping the team member identify key   _____   _____
   factors

2. Helping the team member identify key   _____   _____
   implementation issues

3. Recommending methods for   _____   _____
   implementation

4. Recommending time lines and   _____   _____
   review points

5. Recommending how to evaluate progress   _____   _____

Assessing Your Personal Effectiveness

The end of an intervention is the perfect time to take stock of your personal skills and abilities.

Completing the *Intervention Skills Inventory* in this book is a helpful step. Meeting with the team members after the intervention to receive additional feedback is also very helpful.

What do I personally think are my strengths in making interventions?

_____

_____

_____

_____

What lessons did I learn from this last assignment?

_____

_____

_____

_____

What might I have done differently in this last assignment?

_____

_____

_____

_____

What am I going to do differently next time?

_____

_____

_____

_____

Effective Behaviors When Making an Intervention

Whether you're the team's leader or are being brought in from outside to make the intervention, the following behaviors and practices are essential:

Be serious - Making an intervention requires a serious professional approach. The problem that needs to be addressed is most likely very serious to the members of the team. Regardless of how critical it really is, the person intervening should always behave in a way that mirrors the feelings of the team's members.

Be neutral - It's important to always stay neutral when intervening. You can do this by avoiding all involvement in the tasks of the team. The intervenor should also avoid the temptation to offer the team solutions to their problem. You can offer the team suggestions, but these must never be put forward as 'should' statements. It's also very important not to favor individuals or agree with one side or the other in a conflict.

Be attentive and interested - Make eye contact with the team members at all times and pay close attention to what's being said. Keep your own set of notes and prove that you are listening by summarizing from time to time. Never look impatient or distracted.

Be honest and sincere - Never tamper with survey results or otherwise distort information fed to you. Don't tell one member of the team one thing and give the opposite story to someone else …it'll catch up with you. Don't tell anyone what he or she wants to hear just to make them happy; be prepared to tell the truth especially if members seem out of touch with the facts.

Be up front with the team leader or who ever called you to help; that you aren't there to 'serve' them, but to use tools and techniques that enable the team members to improve the performance of the team.

Be assertive - Making interventions requires high levels of assertiveness. Interpersonal conflicts are often interwoven with the problems the team wishes to discuss. Because member behaviors can get out of hand anytime sensitive issues are discussed, you have to always be ready to make immediate interventions. If you can't be appropriately confrontational, team members won't feel confident delving into their really sensitive issues with you at the helm.

Be well prepared - It's important to spend about as much time designing the final activities as making the planned intervention itself. If it's your first intervention, or a tricky one, spend twice as much time preparing as delivering. Have your data ready, know what you'll say at the onset and have a variety of alternative activities on hand.

Be flexible - Interventions are not like training – they rarely go exactly as planned. Be mentally prepared for this and don't force the team 'back on track' just to stay on your agenda. The saying 'go with the flow' is a good rule of thumb and acts as a reminder to follow the lead of the team. If they seem to need more time to discuss an important issue, it's wise to adjust the agenda so that they can reach a conclusion on that matter before moving on. If they seem totally unwilling to tackle a topic, that may mean this isn't the right time to delve into that particular topic.

Trust the process and the team - If the intervention has been well designed to surface issues and is a good match for the skills of the members, they will find the solutions they need. Anyone making an intervention has to believe in the wisdom of teams and their natural desire to do the right thing.

Common Mistakes and Pitfalls

The following represent some of the most common mistakes to avoid:

1. Giving the team advice on what to do to solve their problem, instead of creating a process whereby the members can work on their problem themselves.

2. Assuming any one person's views about the problem are shared by the rest of the team and, because of that, failing to gather data from all team members.

3. Proceeding with the intervention without checking at the beginning and then again periodically throughout the intervention, to determine how members feel the intervention is going.

4. Allowing the team to move into solving their problem with less than a thorough analysis of their actual situation.

5. Assuming there's group agreement on the problem without checking with each person about how they view the situation. Forgetting sensitive issues need a high degree of commitment and consensus to resolve.

6. Not checking out the intervention activities with the whole group before running them.

7. Not having a clear agreement for the intervention.

9. Defending an intervention that isn't working out.

10. Not having at least two alternative activities in your back pocket.

11. Talking too much; listening too little.

12. Getting drawn into content, taking sides or taking over.

13. Settling sensitive issues 'behind closed doors' when they really need to be settled out in the open.

14. Not trusting the members of the team to know what's right for them.

15. Being biased toward the solutions being suggested by one person because they are in a position of power or you favor them for some reason.

16. Pushing the team to take a risk they say they aren't ready for.

17. Not setting aside the right amount of time and not finding a really private place to hold the intervention.

18. Not using appropriate body language.

19. Using tired sounding phrases like "I hear where you're coming from," instead of speaking in an honest and simple manner.

20. Not being truly sincere in wanting to help the team.

> *Be well prepared • Be neutral*
> *Be totally honest • Be yourself*

Ethical Considerations

Throughout any intervention process, the person making the intervention must pay attention to how they conduct themselves. The following are just a few of the things that should be kept in mind:

- Keep all discussions with the team confidential. Never discuss the team's problems with others.

- If you're going to discuss team information with people outside the team, this must be cleared with the team.

- Never put anything into writing that can't be shared openly with the whole team.

- Never create a situation where team members 'gang-up' on one member.

- Stay calm and neutral, always using appropriate language in sensitive situations.

- Stop an intervention that's becoming negative, vindictive, or is overly judgmental of specific individuals.

- Never become the tool of the leader, senior management, or a friend on the team.

- Don't use the interventions as an opportunity to do what you think is right, follow the process and focus on what members need.

- Never take sides or personally express disapproval of a specific member's actions.

- Withdraw yourself if it's becoming clear that you've lost the confidence of the team members.

- Never conduct an intervention with negative intent. Always strive for a positive outcome.

Notes

Bibliography

Argyris, C. *Intervention Theory and Method: A Behavioral Science View.* Reading, MA: Addison Wesley, 1976.

Auvine, B., Densmore, B., Extrom, M., Poole S., and Shanklin, M. *A Manual for Group Facilitators.* Madison, WI: Center for Conflict Resolution, 1978.

Beckhard, R. *Organization Development.* Reading, MA: Addison-Wesley, 1969.

Bennis, W., Benne, K., and Chin, R. *The Planning of Change.* New York: Holt Reinhart & Winston, 1969.

Blake, R. and Mouton, J. *Consultation.* Reading, MA: Addison-Wesley, 1976.

Block, P. *Flawless Consulting.* San Diego: University Associates, 1981.

Brown, L. "Research Action: Organizational Feedback, Understanding, and Change." *Journal of Applied Behavioral Science,* 8, 1972.

French, W., Bell, C., and Zanack, R. *Organization Development: Theory, Practice, and Research.* Dallas: Business Publications, 1978.

Lawler, E.E. *High Involvement Management.* San Francisco: Jossey-Bass, 1986.

Lippitt, G. and Lippitt, R. *The Consulting Process in Action.* San Diego: University Associates, 1978.

Marguiles, N. and Wallace, J. *Organizational Change: Techniques and Applications.* Glenview, IL: Scott Foresman, 1973.

Reddy, B. *Intervention Skills, Process Consultation for Small Groups and Teams.* San Diego, Pfeiffer & Company, 1994.

Schwarz, R. *The Skilled Facilitator.* San Francisco: Jossey-Bass, 1994.

Schein, E. and Bennis, W. *Personal and Group Change Through Group Methods.* New York: Wiley, 1965.

—. *Process Consultation: Its Role in Organization Development.* Reading, MA, Addison-Wesley, 1988.

An Ounce of Prevention

Whether it's our cars, our homes, or our health, we all know that regular check-ups and preventative maintenance are the best strategies for avoiding breakdown. The same is also true of teams!

Rather than waiting until your team shows signs of trouble, consider implementing the following preventative strategies early on.

Prevention Strategy #1. Conduct a Comprehensive Team Launch

Avoid the temptation to plunge directly into the team's task at the first meeting, without properly launching the team. As outlined on page 42, a proper team launch involves such important activities as: member introductions, creation of a team goal, development of specific objectives, creation of team norms, clarification of empowerment levels, creation of a skills profile, identification of customers, products and services, and development of a communications plan.

Omitting this important step is like asking for storming. Without a strong foundation, a team is prone to on-going frustration and confusion. Lots of teams that get into trouble are there because they were never properly launched in the first place.

You should also keep in mind that launch components go stale quickly. The team's goal can change, members may leave, work may need to be reallocated and so forth. Any time there's a major change, you need to redo the affected team launch components. Even if there are no major changes, every team needs to revisit its parameters at least once a year.

Prevention Strategy #2. Provide Training

Being on a team requires a whole new set of skills for both the members and the leader. A one or two-day training session just before the team gets going is a great idea. There are literally hundreds of excellent teambuilding workshops available from both internal human resources departments and from external training companies.

Among the things teams need are: an understanding of the team concept and the stages of team development, skills in facilitation and meeting management, conflict management, decision-making options, empowerment, and effective team behaviors. Teams also need to know how to use discussion tools like *Forcefield Analysis* and *Systematic Problem-Solving*.

In addition to participating in team training, all leaders should attend some sort of leadership training. Leading a team is different from both supervising staff and managing a department. Successful team leaders need to master the tools and techniques that are unique to this challenge.

If time and cost limitations don't allow for training sessions, the key team learning points should be incorporated into the team launch process or taught by the team leader during the team's regular meetings. A lot of storming can be prevented by providing members with the necessary training!

Prevention Strategy #3. Create and Use Your Team's Norms

Always make sure your team has a set of *norms* that are posted at every meeting.

Team norms are an important tool for managing member behaviors. They should be written up on a large flipchart sheet and posted in the room whenever the team is meeting. Posting the rules empowers members to 'call' each other on poor behavior by pointing out that specific rules are being broken. The active use of norms is the first and most important tool for using peer pressure to control behavior.

Prevention Strategy #4. Anticipate Storming

Another key strategy that helps minimize storming is to teach members about the stages of team development and alert them to the potential for storming. Make sure they understand the signs of storming (page 8) and that this stage is quite normal. Then hold a preventative discussion that creates strategies the team can use whenever storming occurs. Break the team into pairs and ask each partner to think of one or two strategies in response to the following questions:

- *What should we do if we notice that we're starting to experience frustration and dissatisfaction?*

- *What should we do if we start to experience confusion about our goal, roles, and relationships?*

- *What should we do if we start to see interpersonal conflicts?*

- *What should we do if our meetings start to spin in circles without real progress being made?*

- *What should we do if any of us have concerns about the leader?*

When pairs have completed their discussions, hold a plenary to pull together all of the ideas generated and record these on a flipchart. These ideas should then be typed up and distributed to the members.

The significance of this discussion is that it creates awareness and sets the stage for making interventions. By getting the members to answer the questions, they're buying into a strategy of dealing with any problems as soon as they come up. This discussion helps the team members feel they have some control of how well the team functions and sends the message that they're responsible for its health.

Prevention Strategy #5. Identify Team Problems

Instead of waiting for problems to become huge, it's best to identify blocks to high performance early in the life of a new team.

About eight weeks after the team forms, set aside a half hour at a team meeting to identify and then prioritize all the barriers the team is facing using a *Forcefield Analysis* and a *Multi-Vote*.

Create three columns on the flipchart and ask:

1) What' going well?	2) What's getting in our way?	3) Prioritize
What's working for us?	*What's blocking us from being effective?*	*(multi-vote)*

Once the issues have been identified, set aside time at future meetings to begin systematically solving them one at a time. Even if you only work on one problem a month, it's better than ignoring issues until they become major stumbling blocks to the team.

Prevention Strategy #6. Use Peer Feedback

The most powerful tool any team leader can possess to handle member behavior is peer feedback. Within six weeks of launching your new team, you should conduct the feedback process described on page 58. This activity should be repeated at least once every six months.

When feedback is routine, members have the opportunity to proactively tell teammates what they appreciate about each other, as well as share their concerns. This vents problems while they're small.

The power of personal feedback is that members become more accountable to each other. Members who might not be performing as well as they should, are made aware that they're accountable to their teammates. Using peer pressure is known to be the single most powerful means of controlling group behavior. Since it's so simple to use, no leader should operate their team without the regular application of peer feedback.

Prevention Strategy #7. Monitor Team and Meeting Effectiveness

Conduct a *Team Effectiveness Survey*, every six to eight weeks, whether or not the team shows any serious signs of trouble. Use the survey on page 63 or create your own survey questions to suit the situation. You can also alternate the team survey with the *Meeting Effectiveness Survey* on page 66.

Use the *survey feedback* method described on page 61 to surface and address issues. Using survey feedback systematically helps nip problems in the bud and teaches members how to identify and solve their own problems.

Preventative Strategy #8. Implement Team Leader Feedback

The best way of avoiding future power struggles, and adjusting relationships as the team develops through its growth stages, is to hold periodic check-ups on the leader-member relationship. This can be done in two ways.

Approach #1

Members can be asked to anonymously rate the leader by adapting the *Team Leader Assessment Survey* on page 24. The results can then be fed back to the group, who then assess it and prepare feedback for the leader in the following form:

> *"What you do that is really effective - keep doing it!"*

> *"What you could do to be come even more effective."*

Approach #2

The second method is to conduct a *Needs and Offers* session like the one detailed on page 60. This consists of the leader leaving the room while the members discuss:

> *"What we need from you so we can be more effective."*

> *"What we are offering you to support you."*

While waiting outside the room, the leader answers the same two questions. The leader and the members are then reunited to share what they want, as well as what they're willing to offer each other.

These leader-member feedback exercises provide the leader with an opportunity to model gracious acceptance of feedback. It also provides the leader with valuable information about how the leadership needs of the team are changing over time.

Make Interventions Part of the Culture

The capacity to make team interventions is so important that it really shouldn't be left to chance. If team leaders and members learn to make effective interventions and adopt preventative strategies, as per the calendar at the bottom of this page, storming episodes should be few and far between.

If and when team storming does arise it should be regarded as an opportunity for learning and growth. Adopting this mindset and the strategies in this book will hopefully keep your team from ever thinking of itself as a team in trouble!

Preventative Strategies Calendar

The following is a purely hypothetical example of how your team might schedule a year's worth of preventative activities. Construct your own maintenance schedule to suit your unique needs.

Month 1	Month 2	Month 3
•Team leader training •Identify problems •Member training •Team launch session (Anticipate storming)		•Meeting survey
Month 4 •Leader feedback •Peer feedback	**Month 5**	**Month 6**
Month 7 •Update team launch •Team survey components	**Month 8**	**Month 9**
Month 10 •Leader feedback	**Month 11**	**Month 12** •Meeting survey •Peer feedback

Notes

Bibliography

Bolton, R. *People Skills: How to Assert Yourself, Listen to Others and Resolve Conflicts.* Englewood Cliffs, NJ: Prentice-Hall, 1979.

Hargrove, R. *Masterful Coaching.* San Diego, Pfeiffer & Company, 1995.

Kepner, C. and Tregoe, B. *The Rational Manager.* Princeton, NJ: Kepner Tregoe Inc., 1965.

Kayser, T. *Mining Group Gold.* El Segundo, CA: Serif Publishing, 1990.

Mizuno, S. *Management for Quality Improvement.* Cambridge, MA: Productivity Press, 1988.

Nadler, D. *Feedback and Organization Development: Using Data Based Methods.* Reading, MA: Addison-Wesley, 1977.

Nichols, R. and Stevens, L. *Are You Listening?* New York: McGraw-Hill, 1975.

Nierenburg, G., Calero, H. *How to Read a Person Like a Book.* New York: Pocket Books, 1975.

Osborn, A. *Applied Imagination.* New York: Scribner, 1953.

Parker, G. *Team Players & Teamwork: The New Competitive Business Strategy.* San Francisco: Jossey-Bass, 1990.

Rummler, G. and Brache, A. *Improving Performance.* San Francisco: Jossey-Bass, 1990.

Steil, K., Barker, L. and Watson, K. *Effective Listening: Key to Success.* Reading, MA: Addison-Wesley, 1988.

Walton, R. *Interpersonal Peacemaking: Confrontations and Third Party Consultation.* Reading MA: Addison-Wesley, 1969.

Walton, R. *Managing Conflict—Interpersonal Dialogue and Third Party Roles,* 2nd ed. Reading, MA: Addison-Wesley, 1987.

Wolff, F., Marsnek, N., Tracey, W., and Nichols, R. *Perceptive Listening.* New York: McGraw-Hill, 1983.

Sample Planned Interventions

On the following pages, you'll find a selection of sample interventions that reflect many common situations we've encountered in our work with teams. While these intervention designs have certainly been tested in a number of situations, anyone making interventions is advised not to follow them verbatim. We suggest you regard these examples only as learning tools, and that you always gather your own data and custom design any intervention to fit the specifics of your situation.

You'll notice that our examples don't offer timeframes or other meeting details. This is a deliberate omission. We have no way of knowing how many members you'll be dealing with or the seriousness of your team's problems. Please also keep in mind that there are often a number of ways of dealing with any situation. We may demonstrate an intervention with just-in-time training inserted right into a team meeting, while another teambuilding expert might recommend a formal training workshop to resolve a similar situation.

We hope that these examples provide helpful insight into how a teambuilding consultant might structure and handle a particular situation. They'll also help you see how a variety of tools and techniques can fit together to make a whole intervention that helps a team in trouble.

Sample Planned Interventions Index

#1 Resistance to Being on the Team

Situation Description

From the moment that the team was announced, several of the prospective members were overheard telling colleagues that they didn't understand why they needed to be part of a team; they would much rather continue to work alone, as they had for years. Some feared losing their autonomy. Others were concerned about having to go to a lot of meetings and waste time. Still others were worried that being on a team would reduce the amount of recognition they might receive. As time went on members were less and less thrilled to be attending. After the team was formed it met for months without dealing with these issues, even though team performance was noticeably affected.

Intervention Goal

To help members understand the potential of teamwork and gain their buy-in to this particular team.

Step 1: Assessment - Gather Information

The person making the intervention needs to interview each team member individually to gauge how much they know about team work, how committed they are individually to the team and to let them express their concerns in a safe forum. Unless the situation feels overly sensitive, it can certainly be made by the team's leader.

If there's reason to believe that members won't reveal their true feelings, during a one-on-one interview, even to a neutral third party, an anonymous survey may be needed. Both the sample interview questions and a survey for this situation can be found starting on page 91.

Step 2: Planning - Assess the Information and Design the Intervention

In this hypothetical case the interviews and survey revealed that:

• the team members lack understanding about the purpose of the team they were asked to join

• members have never bought into the idea of being on this team

• they also need information about how teams operate in order to dispel member concerns

- specific issues about losing autonomy and not being recognized need to be acknowledged and resolved

- members are having a real problem finding the time to attend team meetings because of workload problems

In terms of the types of team intervention activities needed, this team needs to take the time to conduct a thorough team launch discussion (*Type #1*) which includes getting buy-in from the members. They then need to solve specific problems related to time management (*Type #3*).

Step 3: Contracting - Feed Back the Data and Intervention Proposal

The information gathered from members needs to be put on a flipchart in simple, clear language. The tone used in presenting this data should be totally neutral and without any hint that it's inappropriate for people to have these negative views. Instead, expresses empathy and understanding for these concerns, plus confidence that they can be dealt with successfully.

Feed back the proposed intervention agenda, spelling out its objectives and specific activities. Since members are in a generally resistant mood, be prepared to deal with their reluctance. This can be done by asking them to discuss their reservations about the intervention session and by getting them to identify under what conditions they would be willing to give the session their full support. Since people are more willing to participate in an event they feel they've helped design, be open to member input throughout the contracting session.

Step 4: Intervention - A. Conduct Components of a Team Launch

These folks need to be given an orientation to teams: the benefits and how they function. The members then need to be asked: *"How could we benefit from being a team?"* or *"What areas of our work could we do better if we worked on them together?"* Their response (buy-in) will help members accept the idea of the team. The members then need to be facilitated to create a common goal, identify customers, products and services, create objectives and work plans, clarify roles and responsibilities, and write a set of team norms. For more on conducting a team launch refer to page 42.

As members leave the launch meeting, ask them to complete an exit survey posted on a flip chart at the door. A sample *exit survey* is provided on page 69. This survey asks members to rate how they feel after the intervention and helps the person making this intervention gauge if more work is still needed on this issue.

B. Help Solve Team Problems

The issue of finding the time to attend team meetings needs to be placed on the table. Use the *Systematic Problem Solving Model* beginning on page 52, to facilitate a discussion of the underlying causes of the time crunch, identify solutions, and plan for action.

There are lots of organizations that get into teams without giving people the extra time they need to launch those teams properly and hold regular team meetings. In these situations the person making the intervention may need to go to senior management before the problem-solving portion of this intervention to gain support for removing organizational blocks to teamwork.

Step 5: Follow-up

In cases involving resistance, it's critical that the leader take over responsibility for ongoing monitoring of how people are feeling about being on the team. That means speaking to people between meetings, one-on-one, to find out how they feel it's going. It may also mean using an exit survey at the end of the next few team meetings, to gauge the level of member satisfaction and find out what questions are still unanswered.

Snapshot of this Intervention:

1. Conduct both interviews and a survey.

2. Design an intervention based on the information gathered.

3. Feed back the data and the design to the members.

4. Clarify portions of the team's parameters and help members solve the time management problem.

5. Check on progress on an ongoing basis.

Tools & Techniques

Interview Questions

Some suggested questions for the one-on-one interview session with the members of a resistant team.

What's your understanding of the reason this team has been formed?

Do you consider the team's mission to be important? Why?

Why do you think you've been asked to join this team? What special skills do you bring?

What do you think are the benefits of working together as a team?

What issues/problems/strategies can this team tackle that the members wouldn't be able to take on by themselves?

What changes or accommodations would relieve your time and workload concerns about being on this team?

What do you think might be the drawbacks of being on this team? What concerns you personally?

What questions do you want answered at the team's next meeting?

Survey

Please complete the following survey anonymously and return it as per the information on the cover of the envelope.

1. How would you rate the information you have so far about how this team operates?

1	2	3	4
none	not sure	some	all I need

What questions do you need answers to at the next meeting?

_____

2. How clear are you about the mission of this team?

1	2	3	4
no clue	a few details	some idea	totally clear

3. How would you describe your feelings about being on the team?

1	2	3	4
a waste	not sure	it's okay	enthusiastic

4. What are your main complaints about being on this team?

_____

_____

What do you think are the benefits of being part of this team? What can this team do that you can't do acting by yourself?

_____

_____

5. Why are you having difficulties finding time to attend team meetings? What other pressures or barriers are you encountering?

_____

_____

Exit Survey for Resistance to Being on the Team

As you leave this meeting would you please share your impressions:

How clear are you now about purpose of this team?

1	2	3	4	5
totally confused	still some questions	can't say?	quite clear	totally clear

How committed are you now personally about being on the team?

1	2	3	4	5
opposed	not very interested	not sure	somewhat committed	very committed

To what extent have we solved the problem of not having time for meetings?

1	2	3	4	5
no solution		somewhat resolved		totally resolved

What questions do you still want to have answered about the team or how it functions?

#2 Dysfunctional Behaviors at Meetings

Situation Description

The members of this team have lots of energy and good ideas but meetings are unruly. Members often interrupt each other before they finish their thoughts. There's no evidence of active listening and people seldom build on the points others have made. With people constantly cutting each other off, animosities are growing, and the atmosphere is becoming strained. Because there's a tendency to change topics without finishing discussions, little work is getting done. The team feels like it's spinning its wheels.

Intervention Goal

To help the team identify and solve its team meeting problems and gain the necessary skills to behave more effectively.

Step 1 - Assessment - Gather Information

When a group has become dysfunctional, the best way to understand the interaction dynamics is to observe the members during an actual meeting. The person making the intervention needs to get member permission to sit unobtrusively on the sidelines during a typical team meeting in order to observe the members in action. Using the observation sheets in this section, the observer can track specific behaviors of both individuals and of the group as a whole.

Step 2 - Planning - Assess the Information and Design the Intervention

Observation of the team in this hypothetical case revealed that:

- team members lack basic group and meeting skills

- individuals don't know how to be interpersonally effective

- the team lacks a set of norms that the members can use to maintain order at meetings

- the team leader isn't making immediate interventions to manage either the constant digressions or the ineffective interpersonal behaviors of the members

In terms of the *types* of intervention activities that are required, this team needs to develop and learn to use *norms* at meetings (*Type #1*). The members of this team also need to receive training in interpersonal and meeting skills as a total group (*Type #2*). In addition, the team leader needs to attend facilitation skills training to improve his ability to facilitate assertively in challenging situations (*Type #2*). The team also has specific meeting problems that members need to address and resolve (*Type #3*).

Step 3 - Contracting - Feed Back the Data and Intervention Proposal

Once both the members and the leader have been observed in action, it's advisable to first meet privately with the team leader to give him specific feedback about his need for training. In this scenario, the leader needs to attend both facilitation skills and meeting skills training workshops.

At the contracting meeting with the team, it's best to be sensitive and blend together comments about individuals into general observations that don't single out any one person.

In this scenario the feedback would focus on observations like:

> *"I observed there were four instances when the team moved on to another topic before finishing the conversation in progress."*

> *"On three occasions, members were interrupted in mid-sentence by people who didn't acknowledge the points being made."*

> *"Only three of the eight items on the agenda were completed."*

Once the members have had an opportunity to absorb the feedback and ask questions, the intervention components should be explained. If members seem reluctant, they may need to be asked a series of buy-in question like: *"What will happen if we do nothing about our meetings?"* or *"What can we gain by improving our meetings?"*

If member reluctance seems based on fears (i.e., that the intervention might get personal) it's important to surface these concerns at the contracting meeting and help set *safety norms* for the upcoming meetings.

To set safety norms ask the members:

> *"In what ways could the upcoming intervention make the team's situation worse?"*
>
> *"What rules or conditions would have to be in place before you would feel confident and comfortable in proceeding with the proposed intervention meeting?"*

Record all suggestions and agree to implement all that are feasible.

Step 4 - Intervention - Part A: Help the Team Set New Norms

At the start of the intervention, place the team leader outside the group and ask him to act as the observer for the intervention meeting. Have the leader observe not only the team dynamics, but also the facilitation techniques being used. At the end of the session debrief the meeting with the team leader, focussing particularly on all of the interventions that were demonstrated.

Review the safety norms established at the contracting meeting and set aside about a half hour to help the team add to them so that they end up with a more complete set of team norms. Explain what norms are and give one or two examples. To ensure that everyone participates, have each person choose a partner and give the partners four minutes to come up with at least five rules of conduct that this team needs. Facilitate a discussion to synthesize these points into a set of norms. Post these on a wall in the meeting room

Part B: Train Members in Interpersonal Skills

Next hold a brief training session about effective meeting practices. Review the sheets in this section on *Effective and Ineffective Member Behaviors*. Point out that the team leader will be observing the team in action and will report back on specific behavioral incidences. Hand out the team observation sheets and ask each member to take responsibility for observing and recording specific incidences of their own and other's behaviors throughout this session.

Part C: Help Identify and Solve Problems

Prepare a short one to two page handout about the characteristics of effective meetings. Ask members to look at the description of an effective meeting for comparison and conduct a *Forcefield Analysis* by asking:

"Thinking about this team's last few meetings"...

1. "What are we doing right?"   **2. "What are we doing wrong?"**

When the *Forcefield Analysis* is complete, facilitate a problem solving exercise. Take each of the problems identified in the right hand column #2, one at a time and...

    a. analyze why it's happening and how

    b. brainstorm solutions

    c. generate either action steps or new norms to address each issue. Add all new norms to those already posted.

At the end of this discussion, ask the team leader to share observations about which behaviors were exhibited. Ask team members to offer their observations as well. Ask the team to look at their norms and identify which were conformed to and which were broken. Add any new norms that might emerge through this debrief discussion.

Step 5 - Follow-up

Empower the team to continue to monitor its own inner processes by suggesting they implement the *Meeting Effectiveness Survey* on page 66, in four to six weeks. Advise the leaders to feed back the results directly to the team for discussion and a *"What are we doing right?/wrong?"* discussion similar to the one conducted at this intervention. This will help the team to continue to make improvements.

The team can also implement the *Effective Member Behaviors Survey* on page 157 if member behaviors continue to be ineffective.

Another possible follow-up activity is to have the outside facilitator sit in on a future team meeting, to observe the leader's facilitation skills and give him additional feedback at a coaching session.

Snapshot of this Intervention:

1. Observe the team in action.

2. Design the intervention based on the data gathered.

3. Feed back the data and create safety norms.

4. Create a full set of team norms, provide training and facilitate team problem-solving.

5. Leave behind a meeting survey and offer to give feedback to the leader.

Effective Team Member Behaviors

In order to be really effective, all members of any team need to consistently exhibit certain behaviors during meetings. These include:

Listening actively - looking at the person who is speaking, nodding, asking probing questions and recognizing what they say repeating the key points they made.

Supporting - encouraging others to develop ideas and make suggestions, giving them recognition for their ideas and encouraging them.

Staying on topic - staying focussed and finishing one discussion before going off in another direction.

Building on ideas - not only listening to the ideas others put on the table but actively trying to contribute to develop them further.

Probing - going beyond the surface comments by questioning teammates to help them to uncover hidden information.

Clarifying - asking teammates for more information about what they mean, to clear up confusion.

Offering ideas - suggesting solutions, making proposals, offering new ideas.

Including others - asking another member who has been quiet for their opinion, to make sure no one is left out.

Summarizing - pulling together ideas from a number of people to form a synopsis of where the group is at and what has been covered.

Harmonizing - attempting to reconcile opposing points of view, linking together similar ideas and pointing out where ideas are the same.

Managing Conflict - listening to the views of others, weighing opposing viewpoints, objectively clarifying issues and seeking solutions.

Ineffective Team Member Behaviors

When members of a team use any of the following, they're hurting the team's performance and causing rifts between people:

Interrupting - not letting others finish their points.

Blocking - insisting on getting one's way, being unyielding, standing in the way of the team's progress to get one's way.

Going off-topic - directing the conversation off onto other topics.

Ignoring ideas - failing to acknowledge the ideas of others or failing to help them explore their ideas further.

Criticizing - making negative comments about other people or their ideas.

'Yeah Butting'- discrediting the ideas of others without exploring them.

Withdrawing/becoming passive - deliberately sitting on the sidelines, refusing to contribute and not offering the team personal resources.

Grandstanding - drawing attention to one's personal skills through boasting.

Dominating - trying to 'run' the group, dictating, bullying, or talking too much.

Playing 'devil's advocate' - taking pride in being only contrary.

Emotional arguing - taking differences of opinions personally, attacking others personally and/or trying to win rather than seek solutions.

Team Observation Sheet

At today's meeting, keep track of specific incidents of both effective and ineffective behaviors exhibited by individuals and the group as a whole.

Effective Behaviors	*Ineffective Behaviors*
Active listening:	Interrupting:
Supporting:	Blocking:
Staying on topic:	Going off topic:
Building on ideas:	Ignoring ideas:
Probing:	Criticizing:
Clarifying:	'Yeah butting':
Offering ideas:	Withdrawing/become passive:
Including others:	Grandstanding:
Summarizing:	Dominating:
Harmonizing:	Playing devils advocate:
Managing Conflict:	Emotional arguing:

Effective Member Behaviors Survey

Use the following criteria to assess the behaviors being exhibited by members of our team. *Ratings: 1 = poor, 2 = fair, 3 = satisfactory, 4 = good, 5 = excellent.*

1. Rate how good you think we are at active listening?

   1   2   3   4   5

2. How much supporting and encouraging is there at our meetings?

   1   2   3   4   5

3. How good are we at staying on topic and not digressing?

   1   2   3   4   5

4. How much do we listen to each other's ideas and contribute our thoughts?

   1   2   3   4   5

5. To what extent do we probe and really explore new ideas when they are presented to us?

   1   2   3   4   5

6. How consistently do we ask each other for more information to clarify what's being said?

   1   2   3   4   5

7. To what extent do all of our members offer ideas and suggestions?

   1   2   3   4   5

8. How good are we individually at making sure that everyone is included and gets to have their say?

   1   2   3   4   5

9. How good are we at pulling together our ideas at the end of a discussion to form a concise summary?

1	2	3	4	5

10. When two people disagree, how actively do we try to mediate and help them see the similarities that do exist?

1	2	3	4	5

11. How good are we at managing conflict so that differences of opinion turn into healthy and open debates?

1	2	3	4	5

#3 Lack of Shared Accountability for Goals

Situation Description

In spite of the fact that the team has been in existence for many months, there is still a predominance of 'I' instead of 'We'-oriented behavior. Members talk about *"my project."* They compete for resources and seldom offer to help each other. Lately, important tasks have been falling between the cracks because people are unwilling to take actions that are purely for the good of the team. Everyone's clearly working hardest on the things that will benefit themselves. To compensate for those people who aren't working hard on team tasks, a few members are taking on too much work.

Intervention Goal

To help the team come together to form a cohesive unit in which workloads are evenly shared.

Step 1: Assessment - Gather Information

The person making the intervention needs to interview all of the members of the team individually to uncover member feelings about being on the team and discover whether there's a clear, compelling team goal that members have bought into. Specific questions need to be asked about member attitudes towards sharing responsibility, team rewards and joint work planning. The *Shared Accountability Survey* on page 163 can be used to make the member data more objective and encourage greater candor.

Step 2: Planning - Assess the Information and Design the Intervention

The team interviews and survey in this hypothetical case reveal that this team is operating more like a collection of individuals than like a real team. The predominance of self-centered, rather than team-centered thinking indicates lack of a compelling team goal that all of the members have bought into. The uneven workloads stem from a lack of clear team work plans. In addition there are several real issues that prevent people from shouldering their fair share of team tasks.

In terms of the *types* of intervention activities needed, this team ought to conduct a thorough team launch discussion, including setting team goal, objectives, norms, empowerment levels and work plans (*Type #1*). The team also needs to identify and then solve the problems that keep people from working on team projects (*Type #3*).

Step 3: Contracting - Feed Back the Data and the Intervention Proposal

A concise synopsis of member input should be put on flipchart sheets or hand-outs and shared with the team. Intervention activities that relate to the team formation discussions can then be proposed.

To start off the problem-solving activity, list the barriers that were identified. This list might include things like: lack of clear priorities, lack of equipment, lack of joint accountability mechanisms built into work plans, lack of individual recognition and rewards, lack of clarity about personal autonomy over work, poor communication mechanisms, and so forth.

Briefly outline the problem-solving process that will be used during the intervention. In some situations it's a good idea to get team members to prioritize the list of identified problems during the contracting meeting. This lets everyone know which issues will be dealt with first at the intervention session. It also builds interest and buy-in.

Step 4: Intervention

Part A - Conduct Components of a Team Launch: This team needs to discuss 'what's in it for them' to be a team and then work together to create a clear goal statement. They also need to discuss member skills and learning goals. Next they need to get clear on the specific objectives that will help them realize their goal. Finally they need to be facilitated through a detailed work planning session that encourages them to create fairly balanced workloads. The elements of a thorough *team launch* are outlined on page 42.

Since shared accountability is the heart of an effective team, the team needs to discuss *"How do we make sure our workloads stay evenly distributed?"* The team may also need to openly discuss the prevalence of 'I' oriented behavior and create new norms or strategies that encourage 'We' thinking. At the end of this set of discussions, the team should have a set of norms that promote cooperation and sharing

Part B: Help Remove Barriers to Teamwork

This team needs to use the *Systematic Problem-Solving Model* starting on page 52, to address each of their barriers to effective teamwork. Any new norms that are generated should be added to the list of team norms. All of the action steps proposed should be implemented as quickly as possible.

Step 5: Follow-up

Leave behind a follow-up survey that assesses teamwork and cooperation. Encourage the team to implement this survey in four to six weeks. Call the leader around that time to remind him and offer further assistance if any is needed.

Snapshot of this Intervention:

1. Interview members and conduct a member survey.

2. Assess the information and design the intervention activities.

3. Feedback key points and get members to prioritize the barriers to teamwork.

4. Help the team rebuild its structure to include clear work plans and facilitate while members remove barriers to teamwork.

5. Encourage the team to do a teamwork survey in four to six weeks.

Shared Accountability Interview Questions

1. How would you describe your feelings about being a member of this team?

_____

_____

2. What do you think are the:

   Best things about this team?

_____

_____

   Worst things about this team?

_____

_____

3. How clear is the overall team goal to you?

1	2	3	4	5
not clear clear		somewhat clear		totally clear

4. Are there specific objectives that describe how the goal is going to be carried out?

1	2	3	4	5
no objectives		some objectives		a complete set

5. Are you aware of the skills and learning objectives of the other members?

1	2	3	4	5
not at all		somewhat		completely

6. Are there joint work plans that the members created together, that describe how the objectives are going to be carried out?

1	2	3	4	5
no joint plans		some joint plans		joint plans for all activities

7. Do team work plans place fair and equitable responsibility on all members?

1	2	3	4	5
totally unfair		somewhat unfair		totally fair

8. Describe some of the barriers that keep the members of this team from being able to help and support each other. Be specific about the origin of these problems, (i.e., from members, from the leader, from the organization, from the clients, from the physical surroundings, etc).

_____

_____

_____

_____

_____

9. Describe any interpersonal conflicts and/or team conflicts that are getting in the way of members working together effectively.

_____

_____

_____

_____

_____

10. Describe any attitudes, behaviors, or habits that are getting in the way of the team working together.

_____

_____

_____

_____

_____

Additional Comments:

_____

_____

_____

_____

Shared Accountability Survey

Rate how your team is doing now in terms of how much you support each other and are accountable to each other as a team.

1. This team has a clear goal that we all helped to create and are fully committed to achieving.

1	2	3	4	5
totally disagree	disagree	unsure	agree	totally agree

2. We have clear objectives that spell out exactly how we're going to achieve our goal.

1	2	3	4	5
totally disagree	disagree	unsure	agree	totally agree

3. We have clear work plans that we follow and update regularly, that effectively guide   our joint activities.

1	2	3	4	5
totally disagree	disagree	unsure	agree	totally agree

4. Workloads are either fairly balanced or there are good reasons for when they can't be.

1	2	3	4	5
totally disagree	disagree	unsure	agree	totally agree

5. Individuals put the needs of the team ahead of their own individual needs as members of the organization.

1	2	3	4	5
totally disagree	disagree	unsure	agree	totally agree

6. Members often assist each other, offering both their time and resources.

1	2	3	4	5
totally disagree	disagree	unsure	agree	totally agree

7. We regularly monitor our progress, report to each other and seek feedback from each other about our work.

1	2	3	4	5
totally disagree	disagree	unsure	agree	totally agree

7a. We regularly solve team and individual problems together.

1	2	3	4	5
totally disagree	disagree	unsure	agree	totally agree

7b. List any problems that currently act as barriers to effective teamwork.

_____

_____

_____

8. We communicate very effectively with each other.

1	2	3	4	5
totally disagree	disagree	unsure	agree	totally agree

Additional Comments:

_____

_____

_____

_____

_____

_____

_____

_____

_____

#4 Ineffective Decision-Making

Situation Description

The team seems to be having trouble making decisions lately. Too often lengthy discussions are held to make relatively minor decisions, while extremely important issues are settled in a few short minutes. The team uses voting when they should be using consensus on many of the important decisions. When they do use consensus, quiet people and dissenters are typically ignored. Lots of important decisions are made without enough information on hand. If the issue being discussed is contentious, people tend to argue emotionally. Lately the team's decisions have been coming back to haunt them. When a decision turns out to be wrong, the members argue about who really made the decision in the first place.

Intervention Goal

To share key skills with the team so that decision-making is improved.

Step 1 - Assessment - Gather Information

To get a real sense of how the team operates, it's necessary to sit in on a team meeting as a neutral observer. This is the best approach because members are most likely unaware of what they're doing wrong and hence, would be unable to describe the problems clearly in an interview. The observation sheet on page 167 will be useful.

Step 2 - Planning - Assess the Information and Design the Intervention

Observation of the team in this case reveals that they haven't received any training in decision-making and lack awareness of the six main decision options and when to use each. As a result, the members don't discuss which decision-making method to use in specific situations. The team also seems unaware of how to achieve true consensus, what to do if the discussion spins in circles, or members become angry or withdrawn.

In terms of the type of intervention needed, this situation calls for training in decision-making skills (*Type #2*).

Step 3 - Contracting - Feed Back the Data and Intervention Proposal

Summarize observations about the team's decision patterns on a flipchart. Keep the observations simple and general. Provide the team with a brief summary of the proposed training session.

Step 4 - Provide Training on Decision-Making

This can be done as a formal training workshop or the training points can be inserted into a regular team meeting. The second approach is being presented here. In it, there is some theory input at the beginning of the session, members discuss the pros and cons of the various decision-making methods and then conduct a regular team meeting during which they use their new knowledge to make decisions. The lesson plan and workshop tools for this action learning segment begin on page 168.

Step 5 - Follow-up

Since decision-making is such an important team function, encourage the team to monitor its effectiveness on a periodic basis. In this case suggest that the members implement the *Decision Making Observation Sheet/Survey* from page 167 every four to six weeks until ratings improve.

Snapshot of this Intervention:

1. Observe the team making decisions.

2. Plan the intervention based on the information gathered.

3. Feed back observations to the members and propose a training session.

4. Implement a training session on decision-making.

5. Leave behind a *Decision Making Observation Sheet/Survey.*

Decision-Making Observation Sheet/Survey

Use the following criteria to assess team decision-making effectiveness.

Decision-Making

1	2	3	4	5
The team just jumps into decision-making				The team discusses how it will make decisions

Assumptions

1	2	3	4	5
No checking of assumptions				Assumptions are checked

Voting

1	2	3	4	5
Overuse voting, misuse of consensus				The team uses the right decision method

Listening

1	2	3	4	5
No one builds on ideas of others				There is active listening by members

Openness

1	2	3	4	5
People focus on their own ideas				People are open to each other's ideas

Objectivity

1	2	3	4	5
Points are argued emotionally				Issues are debated objectively

Progress-Checking

1	2	3	4	5
The team never stops to check on progress				The team periodically stops to check on progress

Time-Management

1	2	3	4	5
Use of time is not planned				Time is carefully managed

Participation

1	2	3	4	5
Some dominate, others are passive				There is full and equal participation

Closure

	1	2	3	4	5

Little gets decided   There is true closure on issues

Plans

	1	2	3	4	5

No plans to implement   The team ends up with clear plans

Questioning Decisions

	1	2	3	4	5

There is little questioning decisions once made   People tend to second guess decisions

Decision-Making Training Module

The training intervention to improve team decision-making consists of the following activities:

1. Provide a mini-lecture on the six main decision options available to teams. A handout on this is provided on page 169. Describe only the nature of each decision type.

2. Facilitate a discussion of the pros and cons of each decision tool and when to use each. Use page 172 as a handout. Post these notes in the room.

3. Provide extra input on *consensus* decisions. Hand out the notes on this topic and answer any questions.

4. Help the team to form *norms* that will help them be better decision makers. Add these new norms to the team's regular norms. If the members need prompting, the following questions should help:

> *"What should we do if we find that we are going in circles?"*
>
> *"How do we ensure everyone has a say?"*
>
> *"What should we do if things get heated or emotional?"*
>
> *"How do we ensure we stop and check periodically to make sure our approach is working?"*

Hand out the guidelines for *Effective Decision-Making Behaviors* on page 174 if it seems necessary. Go over the key points.

5. Facilitate a team meeting in which members will need to make decisions. Each

time there's a decision to be made, ask the members which of the decision options ought to be used in that situation. Facilitate using the guidelines shared earlier.

6. Debrief the decision-making activity. *"Was the right tool chosen? What was better? What still needs to be improved?"*

The Six Main Decision-Making Options

When a group needs to make a decision, there are six distinct decision-making methods available. Each of these options represents a different approach. Each has pros and cons associated with it. The decision option should always be chosen carefully to be sure it's the most appropriate method for the decision that is before the group. These six options are: (in reverse order of their relative value to teams)

#6. *Unanimous* - this happens occasionally when there's a solution that's favored by everyone and 100% agreement seems to happen automatically. Unanimous decisions are usually made quickly. They are fairly rare and often occur in connection with the more trivial or simple issues.

Pros   fast, easy, everyone is happy, unites the group.

Cons   too fast—perhaps the issue actually needed discussion.

Uses   all right when lack of discussion isn't vital, hence, on more trivial items. Any complex issues should be decided using a method that fosters more discussion.

#5. *One person decides* - this is a decision that the group decides to refer to one person to make on behalf of the group. A common misconception among teams is that every decision needs to be made by the whole group. In fact, one person's decisions can be a fast and more efficient way to make many group decisions. The quality of any one person decision can be raised considerably if the person making the decision gets advice and input from other group members before deciding.

Pros   can be fast, accountability is clearly spelled out

Cons   can divide the group if the person deciding doesn't consult or makes a decision that others can't live with, lacks both the buy-in and synergy of a group decision.

Uses   when the issue is unimportant or small, when there is a clear expert in the group who should make the decision, when only one person has the information needed to make the decision and can't share it, when one person is solely accountable for the outcome.

#4. Compromise - a negotiated approach applicable when there are two or more distinct options and members are strongly polarized (neither side is unwilling to accept the solution put forth by the other side). A middle position is then created that incorporates ideas from both sides. Through out the process of negotiation, everyone wins a few of their favorite points, but also loses a few items they liked. The outcome is therefore, something that no one is totally satisfied with. In compromises no one feels they got what they originally wanted, so the emotional reaction is often: *"It's not really what I wanted but I'm going to have to live with it."*

Pros   lots of discussion, creates a solution.

Cons   negotiating when people are pushing a favored point of view tends to be adversarial, hence this approach divides the group, everyone wins, but every one also loses.

Uses   compromise is often the only alternative when faced with a strongly polarized group, also when there are two solutions proposed, neither of which are acceptable to everyone.

#3. Multi-Voting - this is a priority setting tool that is useful in making decisions when the group has a set of options before them and rank the options, based on a set of criteria, will clarify the best course of action.

Pros   systematic and objective, democratic, non-competitive, participative, everyone wins somewhat and feelings of loss are minimal, a fast way of sorting out a complex set of options.

Cons   often associated with limited discussion, hence, limited understanding of the options, forces choices on people that may not be satisfactory to them, sometimes the real priorities do not rise to the surface, people are swayed by each other if the voting is done out in the open rather than electronically or by ballot.

Uses   when there is a long list of alternatives or items from which to choose or when applying a set of criteria to a set of options clearly identifies the best course of action.

#2. *Majority Voting* - involves asking people to choose the option they favor, once clear choices have been identified. Usual methods are a show or hands or secret ballot. The quality of voting is always enhanced if there is good discussion to share ideas before the vote is taken.

Pros fast, high quality if used after thorough analysis, creates a clear decision.

Cons can be too fast and low in quality if people vote their personal feelings with out the benefit of each other's thoughts, creates winners and losers, hence divides the group, the show of hands method puts pressure on people to conform.

Uses when there are two distinct options and one or the other must be chosen, to decide items where division of the group is acceptable, when consensus has been attempted and can't be reached.

#1. *Consensus* - involves everyone clearly understanding the situation or problem to be decided, analyzing all of the relevant facts together and then jointly developing solutions that represent the whole group's best thinking about the optimal decision. Characterized by a lot of listening, healthy debate and testing of options. Results in a decision about which everyone says: *"I can live with it."*

Pros a collaborative effort that unites the group, high involvement, systematic, objective, fact driven, builds buy-in and high commitment to the outcome.

Cons time consuming, low quality if done without proper data collection or if members have poor group skills.

Uses the most effective decision process for important decisions where the ideas of the whole group are needed and buy-in from all members is essential. The importance of the decision being made, must be worth the time it takes to complete the consensus process properly.

Decision Types Worksheet

Type	Pros	Cons	When to use it
Consensus			
Compromise			
Voting			
Multi-Voting			
One Person			
Unanimous			

Steps in the Consensus Process

Once a team has decided to use consensus, use the following process:

- ensure that members have the information that is needed to make an effective fact-based decision

- make sure the norms that support appropriate behaviors are in clear view and known to members

- ask members to identify the assumptions that are operating in this situation

- write a clear statement of the decision that needs to be made

- write a second statement that describes what the outcome of the decision process ought to be

- conduct a thorough analysis of the situation and record all relevant facts on flipchart sheets

- make sure that everyone is heard from and that people are using effective behaviors

- once the analysis is complete, start generating solutions using either *brainstorming* or the *nominal group approach*

- create criteria with which to sort the proposed solution ideas and to identify the best course of action

- develop action plans that allow the best solutions to be implemented

Norms that Support Effective Decision-Making

✓ We will listen carefully and paraphrase each other's points.

✓ Wherever possible we will build on each other's ideas.

✓ We will always make sure that the decision making process we use has been carefully chosen.

✓ We will use facilitator's during important decision making discussions.

✓ We will avoid arguing by staying open and objective.

✓ We will make sure that everyone's heard during our discussions.

✓ We won't fold, give in, or flip coins to avoid making tough decisions.

✓ We will test our solutions against some objective criteria to make sure they're sound.

✓ We will create detailed action plans and follow-up.

✓ We will evaluate the long term quality of our solutions to assess how sound they are.

✓ We will periodically analyze our decision-making process and improve remaining weaknesses.

Effective Decision-Making Behaviors

To make any decision process work, group members need to behave in certain specific ways. These behaviors can be shared with the group in advance of any decision making session.

Behaviors that <u>Help</u>	Behaviors that <u>Hinder</u>
Listening to other's ideas politely, even when you don't agree	Interrupting people to promote your personal views
Paraphrasing the main points made by another person to acknowledge their ideas	Not acknowledging the ideas that others have put on the table
Praising other's ideas or giving useful feedback	Criticizing or putting down other's ideas
Building on other's ideas	Pushing your own ideas while ignoring other's input
Asking others to critique your ideas, and accepting feedback	Getting defensive when your ideas are analyzed
Being open to accepting alternative courses of action	Staying stuck on your ideas and blocking suggestions for alternatives
Dealing with facts	Basing arguments on feelings
Staying calm and friendly towards colleagues	Getting overly emotional; showing hostility in the face of any disagreement
Being open about your reservations and concerns	Keeping objections to yourself

Debrief of the Decision-Making Session

After a decision-making session, take the time to assess its effectiveness:

"What did we do really well?"

"What still needs to be be improved?"

"What can we do to improve each problem item?"

Note: The team should repeat the above activity every four to six weeks after periodically implementing the *Decision-Making Observation Survey/Sheet.*

#5 Power Struggles on the Team

Situation Description

While the team is still accomplishing its work goals, there's growing tension on the team. Three meetings ago, two team members challenged the authority of the team's official leader while privately attempting to exert influence over other members. Since then members have begun to choose sides and there are now two distinct 'camps' on the team. A lot of energy is being wasted with this power struggle. The quality of the team's decision-making is also being compromised, because members feel they need to agree with one group or the other.

Intervention Goal

To resolve power struggles on the team so that members work together cooperatively and effectively.

Step 1 - Assessment - Gather Information

Power struggles that divide a team are a serious distraction and need to be resolved. The issues of power and control need to be surfaced a dealt with in a forthright manner so the team can focus its energy back on its work.

To fully understand the issue, interviewing team members individually is the recommended approach because there are likely many sensitive and interpersonal issues that wouldn't be revealed in a focus group or in on a survey.

Because this intervention involves the leader, it must be made by a neutral third party from outside the team.

Team members will need to be assured that their specific comments will be kept totally confidential – a promise that needs to be strictly kept.

The purpose of the interviews will be to determine why the power struggle is taking place. Sample Team Member Interview questions are provided on page 178.

Step 2 - Planning - Interpret the Information and Design the Intervention
Confidential interviews with team members, reveal that:

- members are gaining personal confidence and are getting comfortable with the tasks of the team

- members feel that the leader is controlling and overly cautious

- two assertive team members have been challenging the leader and gaining support from some of the members

- the two emerging member-leaders have a past history of disagreements and tend to clash in the meetings

- these two individuals are each trying to get pledges of support from the rest of the members outside of the meetings

In terms of the *types* of team intervention activities needed, this team ought to engage in two separate feedback exercises (*Type #4*) one between members and the second between the members and the leader. The leader also needs to participate in a coaching session with the person making the intervention (*Type #5*). The two individuals who are engaged in the power struggle need to resolve their past and present rivalry through a conflict mediation session in order to end their competitive behavior at meetings (*Type #6*).

Step 3 - Contracting - Feed Back the Data and Intervention Proposal
This intervention is a sensitive one since it involves interpersonal feelings. Because of the pledges of confidentiality, much of the information gathered can't be reported back to the members as a total group. The feedback needs to be carefully worded and expressed in general terms so that issues are identified, but individual comments aren't revealed.

In this hypothetical case members can be told:

- that members agree that there are control issues between them as well as between them and the leader

- that the members need a way of telling the leader what they need in order to achieve a workable balance of power

- that two individuals on the team need to resolve their relationship as team members

- that the total team needs to engage in a peer feedback exercise

Step 4 - Intervention - Part A: Coach the Team Leader

The team leader should be given the opportunity to receive sensitive personal feedback in a confidential coaching session. This approach gives the leader time to absorb any critical comments before the member/leader feedback session is held.

To protect the confidentiality of members, the feedback given to the leader during the coaching session needs to be given in terms of descriptions of specific incidences. The identity of who made specific comments shouldn't be revealed.

Follow the steps of the *coaching process* outlined starting on page 71. Once the leader has identified an improvement plan, she should be encouraged to present this to the team. This can be done either at the start or at the end of the member/leader feedback session.

Part B: Mediate Conflict

Use the process outlined starting on page 75 to help the two competing team members discuss their past and current differences in a private setting. These individuals need to understand that their continued power struggle will ultimately damage the team.

Part C: Conduct a Leader Feedback Exercise

Set aside enough time to conduct the activity described on page 60 of this book.

Part D: Conduct a Peer Feedback Exercise

Set aside time to conduct the peer review activity outlined on page 58 of this book. At the end of the feedback session, end this intervention by asking members to suggest norms that will help the team maintain a healthy balance. Examples of norms that support effective power relationships are provided on page 178.

Step 5 - Follow-up

The members need to monitor their progress on maintaining effective 'power' relationships.

Snapshot of this Intervention:

1. Interview individual members.

2. Interpret the information to create a design.

3. Feed back a general outline of the data and explain the intervention activities to the members.

4. Coach the leader, mediate the conflict, and conduct feedback exercises.

5. Call on the leader to encourage the team to monitor progress.

Team Member Interviews

When interviewing individual members of the team about their 'power' relationships, the following questions may be useful:

- *How would you rate how the team is functioning at this time?*

1	2	3	4	5
ineffective		satisfactory		very effective

- *What are the reasons for your ratings?*

- *What are the strengths of this team at this time? What's it doing well?*

- *What are the weakness of this team at this time? What isn't it doing well?*

- *How would you describe relationships on the team?...between members? ...between members and the leader? Describe these.*

- *What are current empowerment levels like? Are they clearly defined? Do you feel you have the authority you need to perform effectively?*

- *How do you perceive the leadership of the team leader? What are his or her strengths/ weaknesses? How would you describe his or her approach to leading the team? If you could recommend any improvements, what would they be?*

- *Is anyone else providing leadership to the team? How? Does the team need this leadership? Is the leadership of members encouraged or discouraged by the leader? How?*

Norms that Help to Alleviate Power Struggles on a Team

✓ We will systematically share leadership roles at meetings and on team initiatives.

✓ We will support the leadership efforts of all members.

✓ We will surface our need for more empowerment more openly and before tensions build.

✓ We will provide each other with feedback that is helpful in improving each of our respective leadership capabilities.

✓ Rather than engaging in power struggles, we will express our concerns and take a problem-solving approach with any issues.

#6 Individuals Letting Down the Team

Situation Description

The division of labor on the team is becoming an issue. While most members are working hard to fulfill commitments made to clients and to other team members, two individuals don't follow through on their work plans. They create performance gaps that other team members are constantly having to fill. As a result the team is starting to get a bad reputation. The two people who are letting the team down, act totally unaware and unconcerned about the problems caused by their poor performance. On the contrary, they're often overheard telling other people that they're working too hard. When another team member points out the lack of follow-through, excuses and defensive comments are offered in return. Team members are becoming discouraged and angry at these people.

Intervention Goal

To support the underperformers in improving their personal work habits and to restore effective team relations.

Step 1 - Assessment - Gather Information

Since this intervention is of a sensitive interpersonal nature, the person making the intervention needs to hold individual interviews with each member of the team. As in all matters that relate to personal performance, assurances of confidentiality need to be given at the time of the interviews. Although this intervention is somewhat sensitive, it can be made by the team leader, as long as the leader isn't one of the major contributors to the problem.

It's a good idea to interview the people who are letting down the team last. After having heard the input from the rest of the team, far better probing questions can be asked of them at that point. Very general interview questions for this type of situation are provided starting on page 182.

It's important to note that interviews in this situation will need to be very specific to provide quality information for the coaching activity. The person who will be doing the coaching needs to be able to cite specific situations: what happened, when, the impact of those actions, and the reactions of the members.

Step 2 - Planning - Assess the Information and Design the Intervention

Interviews with the members of the team in this case reveal that:

• One of the two underperformers campaigned hard to get on this team but lacks the background and technical skills of the other members. This person never admits his shortcomings or asks for help.

• The other person who's underperforming has gotten engrossed in a 'pet project' that wasn't supposed to take up much of her time. She shrugs off the concerned comments from other members.

• The team leader has let these two members get away with poor performance for several months.

• The team has very loose work plans. These plans lack specific results statements and deadlines. There's little or no monitoring of progress from meeting to meeting. There are no performance rewards or consequences in place.

In terms of the types of intervention activities needed in this situation, the two underperforming members need individual coaching to improve their performance (*Type #5*). The team also needs to revisit its parameters and create more detailed and accountable work plans. Everyone has to participate in this work planning session and make a serious commitment to adhere to the new plans (*Type #1*). The members also need to engage in a peer feedback session to heighten awareness that members are accountable to each other (*Type #4*).

Step 3 - Contracting - Feed Back the Data and Intervention Proposal

While the general outline of the proposed activities can be shared with the members, the sensitive nature of this situation dictates that the personal performance data concerning the two underperformers be revealed only in the one-on-one coaching sessions.

In these kinds of cases there's often general resistance on the part of the members to participate in the intervention. They may be afraid that emotions will become inflamed or that individuals will be embarrassed in front of the team.

To alleviate these legitimate concerns, create *safety norms* at the contracting meeting. These will help members feel that the activities won't get out of control. Sample safety norms are offered on page 183. Some good questions to ask to get people to suggest 'safety norms' include:

> *"What rules can we agree to so that no one gets offended or hurt at the intervention meeting?"*

> *"What if things do get emotional? What should we do?"*

Step 4 - Part A: Coach Underperforming Members

The two underperforming team members should each be asked to attend separate coaching sessions. Using the coaching process outlined on page 72.

Each person must leave their session with an action plan that will improve their personal performance on the team.

These coaching sessions need to take place before the team's work planning discussion so that the underperformers will be attending fully aware that they need to participate in that session in such a way as to remedy their past performance problems.

Step 4 - Part B: Facilitate the Revision of Team Work plans

The team needs to set aside several hours to hold a special meeting to do work planning. Members need to review their goal and objectives, plus identify the specific results that need to be achieved. They also need to develop a specific system for reporting back to the team on the progress being made.

Since workloads have been uneven, the team should consider ranking all of their tasks using a high = 3 points, medium = 2 points and low = 1 point rating for the following two indicators: *difficulty/complexity* and *time demands*. Once assignments have been given out to members, the relative load on each member can be checked by assigning values to each assignment and adding up the totals.

The team should end this session by identifying some additional, new norms to add to their list. These norms would respond to a specific question:

> *"What do we agree to do to hold ourselves accountable for the plans we have made here today?"*

> *"How do we ensure that all workloads stay evenly balanced in future?"*

Implement any suggestions.

Step 4 - Part C: Conduct a Peer Feedback Session

The members of any team need to know that they are accountable to each other. To reinforce this, conduct a written feedback exercise such as the one recommended on page 58.

Since two members of this team are probably feeling somewhat sensitive, it's advisable to end the written feedback exercise with what is known as a 'strength bombardment.' Here's how it works:

- after members have finished writing comments on each other's sheets, everyone should get their completed sheet back

- pass the completed sheets around the table again, this time only one person's sheet at any one time

- as each sheet is passed every member reads the positive comments they wrote to that person out loud

- keep the sheets circulating until each person has had their positive feedback read aloud

This exercise bombards each team member with positive input, boosting self-esteem, and bringing the team together.

Step 5 - Follow-up

The members of this team should be encouraged to monitor their new work plans and should repeat the peer feedback exercise every six to eight weeks. In addition, the person making the intervention needs to follow up on the coaching session with the two underperforming members to ensure that they're making personal progress.

Snapshot of this Intervention:

1. Interview individual members.

2. Interpret the information and creating a design.

3. Feed back the proposed activity and creating *safety norms*.

4. Coach the two individuals, facilitating a work planning session and conducting a peer feedback session with members.

5. Follow up with the coached individuals, encourage the team's self-monitoring efforts and periodic feedback.

Team Member Interviews

When interviewing team members concerning performance issues, the following questions may be useful. Remember to collect specific information if you will be conducting coaching sessions with underperformers.

- *In what areas is the team performing well?*

- *In what areas is it not performing well?*

- *What are the causes of any team non-performance?*

- *How well is work planned? ...are there clear, detailed work plans? ...do team members create these plans together?*

- *How would you describe the levels of cooperation and mutual support amongst team members?*

- *I understand that there are concerns that not everyone is working at the same level/ capacity? Can you give me examples of specific incidences: what happened, when, the impact, how it was handled?*

- *In what way does the organization contribute to people not being able to do their jobs?*

- *What are some of the blocks you've had to overcome? What blocks are still in the way?*

- *If you could only change one thing to improve how the team does its work, what would it be?*

- *How do people's attitudes and behaviors contribute to the problem of unequal work distribution?*

- *How does the team's leader contribute to this problem? What could he or she do differently?*

- *How do you personally contribute to this problem? What could you do differently?*

Safety Norms for a Sensitive Intervention

Here are some examples of the *safety norms* needed if a team is going to tackle sensitive topics:

- ✓ All ideas are valuable and will be listened to carefully.

- ✓ Anything said here 'stays in the room.'

- ✓ Both people and issues will be handled with respect.

- ✓ All suggestions will be given serious consideration.

- ✓ There will be no retaliation on the basis of anything said in this meeting.

- ✓ No one will personally attack another member.

- ✓ All feedback has to be phrased in a constructive manner and aimed at helping the other person.

- ✓ If anyone feels emotionally stressed, they can call a 'time out' and ask for a break or a change in how the discussion is being handled.

- ✓ Everyone will use 'neutral' body language (i.e., no pointing fingers, no disapproving looks).

- ✓ We will debate ideas not each other.

- ✓ Anyone can point it out if the discussion is going in circles or off track.

#7 *Poor Implementation and Follow-Through*

Situation Description

Pressures have been mounting lately and the team's members are working hard. At team meetings, members make important decisions, and identify follow-up actions. Unfortunately there is a troubling pattern of not following through on these plans. Things get discussed and good ideas are put put on the table, but nothing ever seems to happen.

Intervention Goal

To help the team improve its internal operations so that action plans are effectively implemented.

Step 1 - Assessment - Gather Information

This intervention doesn't appear to have an interpersonal dimension. Since there are few sensitive aspects, the fact finding can be done with the participation of the whole team in a *focus group*.

One approach to the focus group is to use a *Forcefield Analysis* to draw out information about what's supporting the team in its attempts to implement action plans and what's blocking implementation.

Once the blocks have been identified they should be separated by 'type' of block (i.e., inside the team and outside the team). The blocks should also be ranked from minor to major using a *Multi-voting* technique.

1) **What's helping us follow through on our plans?**	2) **What's keeping us from following through?**	**Type**	**Rank**

Step 2 - Planning - Assess the Data and Design the Intervention

In this hypothetical case, the forcefield analysis revealed that there are four major blocks to team follow through: lack of a bring-forward system to track progress, fire fighting, a steady stream of unanticipated crises, lack of adequate access to computers, lack of rewards, or lack of consequences for not following through.

In terms of the types of intervention activities needed, this team should apply the systematic problem-solving model to work through the three last barriers listed above (*Type #3*). The team also needs to take time to work on its operating structure and create a thorough bring forward system to better track its progress (*Type #1*).

Step 3 - Contracting - Propose a Course of Action

Since team members participated in the focus group, they're already aware of the priority issues. The main point of the contracting session is to gain the agreement of members to participate in the planning and problem-solving sessions.

Step 4 - Intervention
Part A: Problem-Solve Priority Issues

Use the *Systematic Problem-Solving Process* beginning on page 52 to address each of the three barriers to implementation. Ensure that the team leaves with a plan to monitor how they manage any action plans that get created.

Part B: Design a Bring-Forward System

Facilitate a review of the team's original parameters (goals, objectives, roles and responsibilities, work plans). Ensure that there are measurable results indicators in place for all major team objectives. Work together to establish a monitoring and reporting mechanism so that the team can keep track of its progress. Then report back. Use the monitoring formats on page 186 may be helpful.

Step 5 - Follow-up

Encourage the team to re-do the *forcefield* discussion in four to six weeks to surface any remaining or new barriers to follow through. The team should also evaluate the effectiveness of the bring forward system at that session.

Snapshot of this Intervention:

1. Conduct a *Forcefield Analysis* to identify and prioritize the barriers to follow-through.

2. Plan for a problem solving session with the team and a session to design a bring-forward/monitoring process.

3. Get team agreement to participate in the sessions.

4. Facilitate the sessions.

5. Encourage the team to monitor the effectiveness of its bring forward system and identify future barriers.

Action Planning Worksheet

Team Goal:

Objectives planned	Actions Expected	Deadlines	Results	Person Accountable

How will progress be monitored? (Written, verbal)

_____

_____

How often should we report on progress?

_____

_____

To whom should we report?

_____

_____

#8 Rejection of the Leader

Situation Description

Individuals on the team have been challenging the opinions and suggestions of the team leader lately. When this happens, the members rally to support each other, so that the leader feels totally out-numbered. Between meetings, task groups meet without the team leader and she's often informed that things are taking place after they're already well under way. Members drop by for advice less and less; increasingly they turn to each other. The team leader feels undermined and 'out of the loop.' The members of this team are starting to tell people outside the team that they don't like or trust the leader any longer.

Intervention Goal

To surface the issues that are dividing the members from their leader and reinstate the leader to a position of effectiveness.

Step 1 - Assessment - Gather Information

This is an extremely sensitive intervention that requires the assistance of a neutral third party. This third party needs to meet privately with the leader, to gain her perspective on the situation, and get a firm commitment to go through with the intervention.

The person making the intervention needs to then interview each member of the team individually. The questions on page 192 may be of help. Each member of the team will need to be given assurances that the leader won't be told who said what. They will need to understand, however, that the leader will receive a combined version of the interview comments made by members, at a confidential feedback session. The members should also be asked to resist the temptation to talk with outsiders about the situation.

Step 2 - Planning - Assess the Information and Design the Intervention

Interviews with the leader and the team members in this hypothetical scenario revealed that:

- the team leader tried to empower the team at the beginning but the team made some poor decisions and took risks that led to major mistakes

- the leader now maintains firm control over key decisions. She makes the members get her approval for most actions and controls the team's access to information

- the leader facilitates all the meetings, never letting members take the lead

- the leader had two of the more vocal members of the team moved elsewhere. When members found out about this behind the scenes manoeuvre, trust levels dropped dramatically

In terms of the *types* of intervention activities needed, this team should engage in two feedback activities (*Type #4*) using both a 360 degree feedback instrument and holding a facilitated leader feedback session. Once the leader has received personal performance information, it's important to support her with coaching (*Type #5*). The team also needs to receive training in systematic problem-solving and decision-making (*Type #2*) to learn how to improve the quality of the decisions they make.

Step 3 - Contracting - Feed Back the Data and Intervention Proposal

Since this intervention is sensitive and personal, most of the information gathered will be blended together and fed back to the leader at a confidential coaching session. What will be shared at the contracting meeting are the general findings that support the need for the various intervention activities.

The members need to accept that the leader will be able to keep the specific results of the 360 degree feedback to herself, but will be asked to present a summary of any action plans she intends to implement in response to the input.

Step 4 - Intervention - Part A: Share Feedback with the Leader

Arrange to meet privately with the leader to share the combined feedback from the interviews and to provide the tabulated results of the 360 degree survey. In order to allow her time to absorb the input, set a date for the coaching session to take place a few days later.

Part B: Train Team Members

Set aside two to three hours to conduct training on decision-making and the *Systematic Problem-Solving Model*. It may be a good idea to take a decision the team had previously made and redo it using the *Systematic Problem-Solving Model*. This will help members see the difference in the quality of their decision using a more systematic approach. At the end of the session, help the team debrief how they made decisions in the past to identify where they might have gone wrong. This discussion may yield some new norms to be added to the team's posted rules.

Part C: Facilitate a Leader/Member Feedback Session

At a separate session, conduct a leader/member feedback exercise using the process on page 60. If the leader feels comfortable and ready to do so, she can share some of the feedback received via the 360 degree survey at this meeting.

Make sure that both parties leave the session with clear actions they can take to improve relations.

Part D: Conduct a Coaching Session with the Leader

Conduct the coaching session after the leader has received all of the input from both the survey and the feedback session. Follow the steps of the coaching process on page 71. Encourage the leader to accept her role in the team's problems. Once the leader has formulated a personal leadership improvement plan, encourage her to share these commitments openly with team members at an upcoming meeting.

Step 5 - Follow-up

Team members should be encouraged to monitor relationships on their own and repeat the leader/member feedback activity in four to six weeks. Offer to facilitate these activities.

Snapshot of this Intervention:

This intervention consists of the following steps:

1. Interview the leader and members.

2. Assess the information and create a design.

3. Feed back the data and gain member buy-in to the design.

4. Implement the 360 degree leader survey and then conduct a leader feedback session. Provide the team with training and coach the leader.

5. Suggest that the team implement the 360 degree survey and the leader/member feed back negotiation in six to eight weeks. Offer to coach the leader after the survey.

Team Leader Feedback Survey

Team leaders need to receive feedback regularly from their members about their performance in the following areas. Once you get to know your leader, review and check off those statements that fairly reflect his or her personal style. If any statement doesn't apply, simply leave that box blank.

1.____ He regularly involves members in decision-making on issues that affect them and their ability to perform well on the job.

2.____ She makes sure that there is a steady flow of information both up and down.

3.____ He treats members as partners and resources.

4.____ In meetings, she encourages all present to participate in full discussions and then arrive at consensus decisions.

5.____ He encourages members to independently find and solve problems.

6.____ When mistakes are made, she refrains from assigning blame – debriefing the activity instead, so we can all learn.

7.____ He periodically creates mechanisms so that people can safely give feedback about his leadership. He lets them know that he appreciates their openness even though he may find their observations disconcerting.

8.____ She regards conflict and disagreement as normal and necessary to a vibrant workplace. She doesn't suppress or ignore it.

9.____ He gives recognition to those employees who do a good job.

10.____ She does not appear to feel diminished because she delegates parts of her authority and responsibilities, or shares decision-making.

11.____ He shares what information he has about the organization, its policies and plans with all employees, except for whatever higher management has labeled confidential.

12.____ When she needs to get our acceptance of a new policy or rule set by senior management, she uses discussion rather than coercion.

13.____ He ensures that all of us are clear about our specific objectives and roles.

14.____ If she does has to impose a decision that is 'unpopular,' she ensures that we all understand the rationale behind the decision and listens carefully to our reactions, despite the fact that she can't alter the situation.

15.____ He spends time with each person at least quarterly to give them specific feedback on their performance and to help them set goals.

16.____ People come to her regularly to discuss their problems.

17.____ He knows the career and learning goals of all the team members and works to get them the training and work experiences they need.

18.___ If she comments on someone's performance, she makes sure that it's done in a supportive and developmental way.

19.___ He routinely evaluates our meetings and discusses how we can improve them.

20.___ About once a month, she looks over the empowerment charts for decision-making and search for ways to empower people further.

21.___ He ensures that there is an up-to-date training needs assessment in place and helps arrange for the needed training. He often designs and runs training sessions himself.

22.___ She doesn't necessarily 'chair' every meeting. She encourages others to manage the meetings. Wherever appropriate, she plays the role of facilitator at staff meetings.

23.___ He puts a lot of emphasis on following through to implement any action plans we have created. There are monitoring systems in place to keep us all on track.

24.___ She is an active sponsor of staff initiatives. She goes on our behalf to senior management and to other departments, to run interference, and remove organizational blocks.

25.___ When people come to him to answer their problems, he helps them figure out what to do. He refrains from jumping in to solve the problem for them.

26.___ She believes that planning is the best defense against constantly having to do fire-fighting on crisis situations, so she works with us to troubleshoot all of our plans.

27.___ He believes in recognizing success and enthusiastically helps us celebrate our wins.

Team Leader Interview Questions

- *What is your assessment of current relationships on the team?*

- *What are some examples of good relations on the team?*

- *What are some examples of strained relations?*

- *How would you describe your current leadership style?*

- *In what ways do you think you have performed well as a team leader?*

- *In what areas do you feel you would most like to improve?*

- *Describe any specific incidences that eroded relations.*

- *What were your actions?*

- *What actions did members take?*

- *What have you tried to do to improve relations?*

- *How did these interventions work out?*

- *How do the members contribute to the current problem situation?*

- *How do you contribute to the problem?*

- *What are your goals for this intervention? What would be the best possible outcome?*

- *What are your concerns or reservations about the intervention? Are there any rules or boundaries you would like to establish?*

Team Member Interview Questions

- *What's you understanding of the need for this intervention?*

- *What are the strengths of this team?*

- *What are its weaknesses?*

- *Describe what you think is this team's major problem?*

- *Can you put on the 'leader's hat' and tell me how this situation looks from her view point.*

- *What actions of the leader that made things better? ...Worse?*

- *Describe the action taken by the team members.*

- *What will happen to the team if there isn't an improvement in this situation?*

- *What would you recommend to remedy this situation?*

- *What's your goal for this situation?*

- *What concerns do you have about taking part in this conversation?*

#9 Key Members Leave the Team

Situation Description

After months of success, the team was unexpectedly thrown into chaos. Three key members suddenly left. When the names of the three replacement members were announced, the original team members felt the best course of action was to quickly put the new folks to work and just barrel ahead to avoid losing momentum. A few weeks after the new members joined, the team leader revealed that he'd be leaving too. This was the final blow for the fledgling team, because the members had developed a great deal of trust and respect for the leader. As soon as the leader departed, the team went into a major slump.

Intervention Goal

To help the team quickly and efficiently integrate three new members and a new leader.

Step 1 - Assessment - Gather Information

This team needs to seek third party assistance to get through this transition. The person making the intervention can get input from the members as a whole group using a *focus group*, since the team's woes aren't of a sensitive, interpersonal nature.

The external facilitator needs to understand the history of the group and get a clear picture of member relations before the three members departed. The questions on page 195 may be helpful in conducting the focus group session.

Step 2 - Planning - Assess the Information and Design the Intervention

The focus session with the members of this case study revealed that:

- The team was just starting to really perform well when the three people were suddenly transferred out.

- The team had been through a major storming period three months ago but had satisfactorily worked out their issues.

- The departing team leader had been very empowering and positive. He had encouraged the members to assume leadership roles and had been an excellent facilitator.

- The remaining members are worried about becoming less productive and want to absorb the new members as quickly as possible.

- The members feel that if they get back on their feet, they can 'stand up' to the new leader and make sure he'll let them continue to have similar autonomy and decision-making power, as did the previous leader.

In terms of the *types* of interventions needed, this team needs to understand that they'll be further ahead in the long run if they stop the action to briefly hold a forming stage meeting to start over. This means setting aside at least one full team meeting to facilitate an abbreviated version of a team launch workshop (*Type #1*). This team also needs to implement a 'new leader integration process' to ensure a smooth transition for the new leader. This feedback exercise creates a dialogue that lays down the building blocks for a positive relationship (*Type #4*).

Step 3 - Contracting - Feed Back the Data and Intervention Proposal

Since the data collection was done in a focus group, members are already aware of the dimensions of their situation. The main challenge at the contracting session will be convincing the team to shift their focus from barreling ahead to stopping briefly to rebuild their structure to include the new people. Gaining buy-in to this re-forming exercise is the main challenge during the contracting phase.

A good question to ask for gaining buy-in at the contracting meeting is:

> *"Imagine that you're going to join a new team tomorrow. What questions would you need to have answered and what discussions would you want to have before you could get down to work and feel at home with the other members?"*

The other task at the contracting session is to review the ten components of a *team launch,* in order to identify which elements can be briefly reviewed and which need to be the focus of a major discussion with the new members involved.

Step 4 - Intervention
Part A: Conduct the Components of a Team Launch

The team needs to set enough time on the day the new members arrive to review its parameters and update its team charter to reflect the inclusion of the new people. The 10 components of a team launch are outlined on page 42. This should take much less time than the original launch process. Some elements like the team goal and objectives might only need to be explained to the new members, while other elements like team member profiles, skills, roles and responsibilities might require discussion. This re-launch meeting needs to be a warm and welcoming session that allows the new members to get to know each other and build trust and comfort with the existing team.

Part B: Integrate the New Team Leader

Just before the new leader arrives, the external facilitator needs to meet first with the team, then with the new leader to gather information about their mutual expectations of each other.

The person making the intervention then facilitates a meeting of the two parties in which the relationship of the team and its new leader are negotiated. This activity is described in detail on page 196.

Step 5 - Follow-up

This team needs to monitor relationships carefully and conduct periodic feedback exercises. The members could conduct a *peer feedback evaluation* four to six weeks after the intervention to make sure that members are working to support each other. The team leader could implement a 360 degree leader survey (page 24) or hold a member/leader negotiation session (page 60), at about the same time. A third party facilitator may be useful in conducting any of these activities.

Snapshot of this Intervention:

1. Conduct a focus group to surface issues.

2. Assess the information and create a design.

3. Help the team accept the need to engage in a forming exercise.

4. Relaunch the team and conduct a new leader integration process.

5. Encourage the team to continue to monitor its progress.

Focus Group Interview Questions

- *Tell me the story of your team: when did it start, what's its goal, what stage of team development is it currently experiencing, etc?*

- *Has the team ever experienced a storming period? What was going on?*

- *What was done to overcome storming?*

- *Describe relationships on the team, ...between members, ...with the leader, ...with other teams, ...within the organization?*

- *What's the impact of losing members now?*

- *What is your strategy for integrating the new members?*

- *If you were about to join a new team, what would you need to know about the team and the members before you could function effectively?*

- *What sorts of activities or discussions would make you feel welcome if you went to join a*
- *new team tomorrow?*

- *Describe the style of the departing leader?*

- *What's the impact of losing the leader now?*

New Team Leader Integration Process

A new team leader will be accepted into an existing team more quickly if properly integrated. Below are the suggested steps of this process.

Step 1 - The Team Prepares a Profile

The neutral third party making this intervention meets with the team members before the new leader arrives. Without the new leader present, they respond to the following questions to build a profile of themselves to be given to the new leader.

- *Who are we (i.e., our goal, our members, our objectives, etc.)?*

- *What's our greatest strength as a team?*

- *What's the achievement we're most proud of?*

- *What are we still working to improve?*

- *How have we handled team conflicts in the past?*

- *What could we do if conflict engulfs the team in the future?*

- *How would we describe our current level of empowerment?*

- *How would we describe the leadership style that would work best to keep us growing and working effectively (what do we need from the new leader)?*

- *What we are offering the new leader in return for what we want and need.*

- *Our biggest worry about the new leader is...*

- *Our most pressing question for the new leader is...*

Step 2 - The Leader Prepares a Profile

Once the team has completed its profile, it's sent to the new leader to read in private. The new leader then has a few days to prepare a personal profile that mirrors the one developed by the team. The specific questions to the leader would be:

- *Who are you (i.e., past jobs, history with teams, personal objectives,etc.)?*

- *What's your greatest strength as a leader?*

- *What's the achievement you're most proud of?*

- *What are you still working to improve?*

- *How would you describe your current leadership style?*

- *How would you work with this team given the level of empowerment they've been accustomed to?*

- *What leadership behaviors do you think contribute to overall team effectiveness?*

- *What do you think we should do if conflict arises?*

- *What's your response to what the team wants and needs from you?*

- *What's your reaction to what they're offering?*

- *What are your wants and needs from your new team?*

- *What are you offering them in return?*

- *What's your biggest worry about joining this new team?*

- *What questions do you want to have answered by the new team?*

Step 3 - Facilitate a New Leader Integration Meeting

The person making the intervention facilitates a meeting at which the leader is introduced and shares the answers to his or her questions. Both parties compare notes until all of the topics have been mutually explored to the satisfaction of both parties. The facilitator records areas of agreement and also areas of difference.

Each of the areas of difference should be discussed to identify ways of closing any gaps that exist. The parties need to commit to implementing any action plans they create. This discussion will also yield norms that should be added to the team's norm set.

By the end of the new leader integration session, the leader and the members have had an opportunity to explore sensitive issues and pro-actively define their new relationship.

#10 Rejection of One Member

Situation Description

At first glance the team seems to be doing fine. Closer observation reveals that the team is shunning one of its members. The newest addition to the team had been welcomed at first, but lately no one's speaking to her. No one offers to help her even if she directly asks for support and no one wants to work on projects with her. People even ignore her comments at meetings. While it hasn't degenerated into open hostility, the team's newest member is definitely on the outside looking in.

Intervention Goal

To re-establish effective team relations and rebuild an atmosphere of teamwork and trust.

Step 1 - Assessment - Gather Data

This is a very sensitive situation that requires a great deal of confidentiality. As long as the problem doesn't stem from the relationship with the leader, the team leader can make this intervention.

Since the issue is personality based, the data gathering has to be done in private, through individual interviews. Interview the person who is being shunned first, to get his or her perspective on the situation. This will let you determine whether or not they're aware that there's a problem and how serious they think it is.

The other purpose of this interview is to get the rejected member's buy-in to the idea that you'll be making an intervention into this rather sensitive situation. Be sure to raise all of the very legitimate concerns that the person may be feeling about taking part in an intervention. These concerns are understandable and need to be addressed. The outline on page 201 may be of help in conducting this interview.

The next step is to interview the other members of the team one at a time. The best approach for these interviews is to be totally non-judgmental and ask 'open-ended' questions that encourage each member to describe their understanding of the current situation as it has developed. The members need to be asked to maintain strict confidentiality about these conversations. Unnecessary rumors at this stage will only hurt the team's chances of overcoming its problem.

Step 2 - Planning - Assess the Data and Design the Intervention

From the confidential interviews with team members in this case, you learned that:

• The member being shunned went to a senior manager during a problem with a team project and shared confidential team information. As a result management took the project away from the team, which caused a major loss of trust among members. This issue was never put on the table to be resolved.

• The shunned member is seen as an 'I' person rather than as a 'We' person. Members cited specific examples of situations in which she competed with other members and refused to offer help when they asked her to assist with deadlines.

• In her interview, the shunned member acknowledged that she was being shut out but claimed she had no idea why this was happening.

In terms of the *types* of intervention activities needed, this sensitive situation calls for a initial coaching intervention (*Type #5*), followed by a peer feedback session four to six weeks later (*Type #4*).

Step 3 - Contracting - Feed Back the Data and Propose an Intervention

Since the data collected is sensitive, it should *not* be copied onto a flipchart or discussed in front of the whole group. Instead, prepare only a few sentences to summarize the situation and give support to the proposed intervention activities.

Since everyone on the team is probably well aware of the situation, use the time at the contracting session to establish safety norms for the intervention itself. Refer to page 113 for information about creating *Safety Norms*.

Step 4 - Conduct a Coaching Session

Conduct a private coaching session with the rejected member. Use the process on page 72. Since this person is either unaware of the situation or is in denial, it's important to write out the feedback so they can take it away with them. Help them understand and accept that this is what the other members of the team have reported. Relay the specific details of all past incidents and the impact each had on the members and the team as a whole.

It may be a good idea to stop the coaching session once the feedback has been shared, to give the person some time to absorb it and come back to complete the intervention. During this recess, ask the person to identify what she needs to do to re-establish effective relations with the team.

When the coaching session resumes, build on any ideas she has come up with. Offer your suggestions and help her formulate an action plan.

Now comes the hard part: the rejected member needs to share her plan in order to improve relations with the rest of the team. Her plans to make amends won't heal the team's wounds if they're never shared. There are two options for doing this, depending on the maturity of the team and the emotional resilience of the rejected member. It can be done either out in the open at a team meeting or the rejected person can schedule individual chats with each person.

Whichever approach is chosen, there needs to be guidelines in place to ensure that this discussion doesn't lead to blaming and conflict escalation. Here is the engagement process:

1. The rejected person will repeat a brief summary of the feedback

2. The other member(s) will listen actively without showing negative body language

3. The rejected member asks if there's any other information she needs to know

4. The other member(s) can offer any further information they feel she needs to know

5. The rejected member then presents her action plan to reinstate relationships

6. The other member(s) offer support

Step 5 - Follow-up

In this case the team should conduct a written peer feedback exercise within six to eight weeks of the intervention to make sure the lines of communication are staying open. Use the peer feedback process outlined on page 58.

Snapshot of this Intervention:

1. Interview the rejected member and then the rest of the team.

2. Interpret the information and create the intervention plan.

3. Feedback general information that supports the need for the intervention and explain what will take place. Create safety norms.

4. Conduct the coaching session and then facilitate the whole team session or provide guidelines for the individual meetings.

5. Conduct a written peer feedback exercise in four to six weeks.

Interview Questions for the Rejected Person

To get the impressions of the shunned person, keep the interview session totally open-ended. Letting the other person talk will reveal their level of awareness about the situation and how much they're admitting.

Remember that this is a probing exercise. This is not the time to confront the person with a lot of half-developed rumors. This first interview may end with him or her maintaining that everything is fine and that he or she is not aware of any problems.

You'll only be able to make them face the facts once you've gathered them in the follow-up interviews with team members. For now just let the person talk.

- *How would you describe how the members of this team are getting along with each other right now?*
- *What's the best thing about being on this team for you personally?*
- *What's the worst thing for being on this team personally?*
- *Tell me about your relationships with members?*
- *Have there been any incidents that have affected your relations with the members?*

At the end of the session, you do need to make the person aware that there is a serious problem with relations and that you'll be interviewing the other members of the team. Share the goal of the intervention. Ask him or her what concerns they might have about this activity and what assurances they need from you to protect their emotional safety.

Interview Questions for the Team Members

Your aim at these sessions is not to gossip about the rejected member or assassinate their character, but to gather feedback for a coaching session, resulting in improved team relations with that member. Ask members:

- *How do people on this team generally get along? Is there anyone who is being treated differently by the team?*
- *Describe the coolness you have observed regarding the person in question.*
- *What was the event or events that precipitated this situation?*
- *Exactly what happened, when, how often?*

- *What were the impacts of these actions?*

- *Was the incident pointed out to the person at the time? If so what was their reaction?*

- *Have any efforts been made to surface the issues, offer feedback or seek solutions? What were the outcomes of these efforts?*

- *What advice or solutions would you offer this person?*

The team members need to support this intervention by maintaining total confidentiality and discretion. That means keeping the interview information to themselves and not approaching the rejected person to discuss the intervention while it's under way.

#11 Lack Empowerment & Organizational Support

Situation Description

The team has been operating for several months. At first, members weren't sure they liked the idea of being on a team, but success on a major customer service project cemented the members into a unit. Ready to tackle more ambitious goals, the team members were shocked a few months later to find that their proposals and initiatives were being rejected by management.

Their requests for larger budgets, more staff, and training were all rejected too in spite of the fact that they had just saved the company three times what they were requesting. The members were furious and really started to question if the organization was sincere about the whole 'team thing.'

Intervention Goal

To support the team in creating a detailed empowerment plan and negotiating for increased empowerment with management.

Step 1 - Assessment - Gather Information

This intervention needs to go beyond the team's boundaries and is appropriately made by the team's leader. The leader needs to start by facilitating a discussion with the total team to analyze the current situation and identify the specific incidents where organizational support was refused.

The leader then needs to interview the various members of the management team who refused the team's requests to gain an understanding of why this occurred. The team leader may also need to interview other team leaders, customers and suppliers to develop a profile of the team's capabilities.

Step 2 - Planning - Assess the Information and Design the Intervention

Interviews and team analysis revealed that:

• The team had made a proposal to shorten the internal order fulfillment process by several steps, but had done so without the participation and buy-in of two other teams who would have been directly affected by the change and who objected to the proposal.

• Senior managers are reluctant to give this new team too much authority to make drastic changes since the team has only been functioning for a few months.

• The organization has a history of making decisions at the top and is slow to change.

• The team members are oblivious to the fact that they contributed to the low empowerment situation by working in isolation from other teams, and assuming they were empowered when they really weren't.

This team is working in an empowerment vacuum in which decision-making authority is unclear. The team needs to discuss their empowerment needs and develop strategies to encourage the organization to provide support (*Type #1*) Empowerment planning is a component of a thorough team launch and should have been in place when this team was started.

The team leader then needs to conduct an inter-team session with the other teams affected by the proposed process improvement initiative. This session would aim at gaining the support of the other team for the proposed changes. A major feature of this joint planning session, would be to engage the other team in identifying barriers to change then jointly resolve these (*Type #3*).

Finally the team leader needs to play the role of boundary manager to approach senior management with the team's empowerment plans and their specific requests for raising empowerment levels on specific activities (*Type #6*).

Step 3 - Contracting - Feed Back the Data and Intervention Proposal

Team members need to hear the views of senior management and the leaders of the two teams that objected to the failed proposal to shorten the order fulfillment process. They should be encouraged to accept this feedback and understand that their lack of empowerment stems at least in part, from their image as being unready to handle power responsibly.

The intervention proposal should be explained so that members are comfortable with it and in a positive frame of mind to meet with the other players.

Step 4 - Intervention - Part A: Create a Clear Empowerment Plan

The team leader needs to explain the four level empowerment chart to the members. Refer to the empowerment chart on page 206. Everyone needs to understand that any decision can be made at one of four different levels:

Level I - management makes the decision then informs employees

Level II - management gets input, but then makes the decision

Level III - team members can recommend a course of action, but need managerial approval before implementing

Level IV - team members can make a decision and act on their own

The team needs to examine specific activities and identify both their current empowerment level and the level they would like to be operating at. The team then needs to discuss:

- *Which activities do we need increased empowerment for?*

- *Why do we need this higher empowerment level?*

- *Why might senior management balk? What could go wrong? What would their concerns be?*

- *What checks and balances can we put into place to make them feel confident in empowering us for this specific activity?*

The plan the team develops forms the basis of the negotiations with senior management.

Part B: Facilitate a Meeting with the Other Teams

Next, bring in the other teams to discuss the rejected process improvement proposal. Acknowledge up front that the team had done this without proper consultation. Clarify that the goal of this session is to make amends, improve relations, bring the other teams into the loop and jointly remove blocks to implementation. A brief outline of this session is provided on page 206.

Part C: Mediate on Behalf of the Team

Once the team has created a clear empowerment plan and repaired its faulty process improvement initiative, the team leader can approach the senior managers who were interviewed earlier.

At these meetings, the leader can present what the team learned from its past mistakes. The leader can also review the specific initiatives the team is hoping to take in the near future and negotiate for the empowerment levels the team feels that it needs in order to be able to operate effectively.

If the pre-work is done properly, this presentation should include:

- the empowerment levels the team is hoping to work at on specific activities

- the risks inherent in each activity

- details of how the team will handle all risks

- information about how the team will monitor itself to avoid making mistakes

- a set of results indicators and a critical path for proposed activities

- details of how the team will report to the senior management group on progress

Step 5- Follow-up

Once increased empowerment has been given to the team, it needs to report on progress regularly to senior management. The team also needs to keep its empowerment charts up-to-date, and negotiate increased empowerment for future activities.

Snapshot of this Intervention:

1. Gather information.

2. Assess the information and create a design.

3. Feed back the data and intervention proposal.

4. Create a clear empowerment plan, facilitate a joint meeting of the two conflicting teams and mediate on behalf of the team with senior management.

5. Encourage the team to continuously update its empowerment plans.

The Empowerment Continuum

		Employees Control	
Management Control			
I	**II**	**III**	**IV**
Management Decides, Then Informs Staff	**Management Gets Staff Input Before Deciding**	**Employees Decide & Recommend**	**Employees Decide & Act**
• Telling	• Selling	• Participating	• Delegating
• Directing	• Coaching	• Facilitating	• Liaising
• Management is accountable and responsible	• Employees' ideas harnessed as input to decisions	• Accountability is clearly shared	• Employees are accountable and responsible
• Team members are told about decisions	• Team members are consulted and have input into decisions	• Team members must consult management before acting to get approval	• Team members can set direction and take action without approvals

Process for the Meeting with the Other Teams

Purpose of this Meeting:

✓ To review the proposal to reduce the steps in the order fulfillment process.

✓ To review mistakes made in how the proposal was created.

✓ To gain input and participation from partner teams.

✓ To make a new, joint proposal.

✓ To identify blocks and remove barriers to implementation.

Meeting Agenda:

1. Introduce the purpose of the session.

2. Review the history of how the proposal was put forward and the lessons learned from not involving others.

3. Review the process changes and get input from the other teams (i.e., what they like, what they are concerned about).

4. Review each concern in detail and use *Systematic Problem-Solving* to analyze issues and find solutions.

5. Make changes to the proposal as per the input received.

6. Formulate a plan for putting forward the revised proposal for approval.

7. Discuss how the teams will work together in the future.

#12 Inter-Team Conflict

Situation Description

A few months after the CEO announced a huge bonus for the team that turned in the largest dollar savings through work process redesign, a small war erupted. Two teams that worked side-by-side without incident suddenly started clashing. First they competed for computer time, then one team tried to steal a key customer from the other. At the worst point in the conflict, the teams were even fighting over who had access to the main meeting room. While some element of competition between teams can be healthy, the conflict surrounding these two teams was so intense that it rendered them both totally ineffective.

Intervention Goal

To help two rival teams overcome their differences and build a positive working relationship.

Step 1- Assessment - Gather Information

Since this situation has involved the team's leaders in the conflict, the intervention should be made by an outside, neutral person who is not a member of either team.

The person making the intervention needs to start by interviewing each of the team leaders separately. The next step is holding separate focus groups with each of the teams to get their views of the conflict situation.

Since this conflict extends beyond each of the the teams, it may be a good idea to interview other people in the organization who have knowledge of the conflict.

Step 2 - Planning - Assess the Information and Design the Intervention

Interviews with the two teams in this hypothetical conflict revealed that:

- Team #1 had the mandate to supply a major customer, but Team #2 decided they were justified in also servicing that account because they had provided that customer with products in the past.

- When Team #1 overspent the computer budget, Team #2 assumed they were acting in retaliation.

- Team #2 next sought approval to take over the main board room for six weeks to use as a special project 'command center' without consulting with the other team

- In the midst of Team #2's special project, the leader of Team #1 asked senior management for permission to draft a key member of Team #2.

- When members of the two teams encountered each other in the halls, they either avoided speaking or dropped negative comments in passing.

- Throughout these incidents, the two leaders didn't try to meet to settle their differences. Any communications between them were in the form of curt messages and each one tried to get the support of at least one senior manager for their side of the building conflict.

In terms of the *types* of intervention activity needed, this situation calls for an inter-team conflict *mediation (Type #6)* to work out the past conflict and re-establish an effective working relationship. The two teams need to end their mediation session with a feedback exercise called a *Needs and Offers Negotiation (Type #4)*.

Step 3 - Contracting - Feed Back the Data and Intervention Proposal

Once the interviews are complete, the person making the intervention needs to inform each group separately of the need for the mediation. The actual data collected in the two separate focus groups should not be shared until the actual mediation session occurs.

Both teams need to buy-in to the idea of the mediation and commit to abide by whatever outcome is agreed to.

If members seem reluctant to attend the mediation, they will need to buy into the activity. Ask them:

> *"What will happen if we do nothing to resolve this situation?"*

> *"What are the benefits of re-establishing positive relations?"*

Use the two separate contracting sessions to explain the rules of the conflict mediation exercise to each group and get their input to the norms for that session. Ask members:

> *"What rules do we need to put in place to make sure the conflict doesn't actually get worse during the mediation session?"*

Bring each set of rules to the mediation and check off all the ones that both parties agree to abide by. Enforce these throughout the mediation.

Step 4 - Intervention - Facilitate a Conflict Mediation Session

Set aside at least three hours to conduct this sensitive session. Refer to the *Inter-Team Mediation Process* outline on page 78.

Once the main mediation activity has resulted in detailed action steps, engage the two teams in a *Needs and Offers Negotiation*. This activity lets members ask for and offer the intangible things that might not emerge from a problem solving exercise. It consists of the following:

- each team identifies what it needs from the other team in order to improve relationships

- each team also identifies what it's offering the other team in return

- the two teams then hold a joint discussion to share their respective needs and offers

- both teams commit to accepting the comments of the other team

Ensure that both teams leave the mediation with specific actions to improve future relations.

Step 5 - Follow-up

The teams should come back together briefly in four to six weeks to review the commitments that were made and to assess their joint progress.

Snapshot of this Intervention:

1. Gather information from the team leaders and focus groups.

2. Assess the information and create a design.

3. Feed back the mediation proposal.

4. Facilitate an *Inter-Team Conflict Mediation*.

5. Bring the teams back together to assess how the mediation improved relations.

Notes

Bibliography

Avery, M., Auvine, B., Streibel, B., and Weis, L. *Building United Judgement: A Handbook of Consensus Decision Making.* Madison, WI: The Center for Conflict Resolution, 1981.

Belasco, J. and Stayer, R. *Flight of the Buffalo.* New York: Warner Books, 1993.

Block, P. *The Empowered Manager.* San Francisco: Jossey-Bass, 1990.

Buchholz, S. and Roth, T. *Creating the High Performance Team.* New York: John Wiley, 1987.

Conner, R. *Managing at the Speed of Change.* New York: Villard Books, 1995.

Covey, S. *Principle-Centered Leadership.* New York: Simon & Schuster, 1990.

Daniels, W. *Group Power: A Manager's Guide to Using Meetings.* San Diego: University Associates, 1986.

DePree, M. *Leadership is an Art.* New York: Doubleday, 1989.

Fisher, R. and Ury, W. *Getting to Yes.* New York: Penguin Books, 1991.

Fox, W. *Effective Group Problem Solving.* San Francisco: Jossey-Bass, 1987.

Frank, M. *How to Run a Meeting in Half the Time.* New York: Simon and Schuster, 1989.

Haynes, M. *Effective Meeting Skills: A Practical Guide to More Productive Meetings.* Los Altos, CA: Crisp Publications, 1988.

Kouzes, J. and Posner, B. *The Leadership Challenge.* San Francisco: Jossey-Bass, 1987.

Locke, E. and Latham, G. *Goal Setting.* Englewood Cliffs, New Jersey: Prentice Hall, 1984.

McCall, M. and Kaplan, R. *Whatever It Takes: Decision Makers at Work.* Englewood Cliffs, New Jersey: Prentice Hall, 1985.

Miller, W. *The Creative Edge.* Reading, MA: Addison-Wesley, 1990.

Nadler, G. and Hibino, S. *Breakthrough Thinking: Why We Must Change the Way We Solve Problems.* Rocklin, CA: Prima Publishing, 1990.

Parker, G. *Team Players & Teamwork: The New Competitive Business Strategy.* San Francisco: Jossey-Bass, 1990.

Vaill, P. *Managing as a Performing Art.* San Francisco: Jossey-Bass, 1989.

Van Gundy, A. *Techniques of Standard Problem Solving.* New York: Simon & Schuster, 1989.

About the Author

Ingrid Bens is a consultant and trainer whose primary areas of focus are conflict management, team building, facilitation, leadership, and organizational change. Ingrid has a master's degree in adult education, and over twenty years of experience facilitating team implementation and process improvement in the public, private, and non-profit sectors.

Ingrid also teaches in-house workshops for clients, and makes presentations at conferences for the University of North Texas' Center for the Study of Work Teams, the Association for Quality and Participation, Linkage Incorporated, and the Banff Center for Management. She is a partner in Participative Dynamics, a consulting firm with offices in Sarasota, Florida, and Toronto, Canada.

About the Editor

Michael Goldman is a partner in Participative Dynamics, and has acted as a course designer, trainer and facilitator for many Fortune 500 companies. Michael has a Masters Degree in Health Sciences, specializing in communication disorders and is a certified mediator.

Other Books by Ingrid Bens*

Facilitating with Ease!

A comprehensive guide to the practice of facilitation. Helps build skills in managing conflict, building consensus, listening and running effective meetings. A great resource that's easy to read, yet full of helpful strategies, tools and worksheets. **Code: 4286P**

Facilitation at a Glance!

A condensed, pocket-sized version of the popular manual *Facilitating with Ease!* This guide contains all the tools, techniques, and checklists you need to facilitate meetings. Code: 1062E

*Both of these books are available from GOAL/QPC. Visit our website www.goalqpc.com for more information.